Praise for *Valor 2 Victory*

"The stories will touch your heart. The "advice" will help you understand how to help a loved one through a traumatic event. *Valor 2 Victory* is like no other book out there. Not only do the stories allow you to see through the eyes of those who have suffered personal tragedy, you also get to hear these survivors tell you what is needed to help someone who is hurting emotionally and physically. *Valor 2 Victory* is a must read, and a blessing to those who have experienced trauma and those of us desiring to love them through it."

—Kimberly Chenier
Attorney, Expert Business Advisor, and Author

"*Valor 2 Victory* is a courageous collection of deeply personal accounts that show how truly strong the human spirit can be. Despite traumatic and challenging circumstances, these ordinary individuals arise as extraordinary heroes who face their fears head on. This is an empowering text that will encourage survivors and those who support them through their journey to healing. Thank you, authors, for sharing your heart, struggle and victory."

—April Mosby
Professor, Teacher, and Editor

"This book is excellent and exceeded all my expectations. It is well written and provides a backdrop for overcoming life's obstacles."

—L.C. Green, Jr.
Author, Business Advisor, and Entrepreneur

"This is a powerful yet soft piece of literature that is a must read. Not just by those who have had near-death or traumatic experiences but to those who encounter those who have had those experiences. Jesus asked the question, "When I was hungry, did you feed Me? When I was homeless, did you give Me a room? When I was thirsty, did you give me something to drink?" The reply was, "When did we see you?" We see people every day who are just trying to hold on.

This book scratches an itch in our souls that needed to be scratched. There are many people that are left by the side of the road just left to die in the loneliness of their sorrow and despair. We need healthy reminders like this to reach out to those who are walking with feeble legs and pull them up.

Vivica has a storyline that opens eyes and shut mouths. It's a call to action and it's about time."

—Charles Belvin, Senior Pastor of Lakewood Church International, Teacher, and Coach

VALOR 2 VICTORY

Removing the Drama from Your Trauma

Foreword by Kenneth Mulkey

Ms. Vivica

PRAZEUP INC.

Copyright © 2017 by Ms. Vivica.

All rights reserved. No part of this book may be reproduced or transmitted in any form or by any means, electronic or mechanical, including photocopying, recording, or by any information storage and retrieval system, without permission in writing from the publisher.

Published by
PRAZEUP INC.
www.prazeup.com
eMail: msvivica@prazeup.com

Printed in the United States of America

ISBN: 978-0-9724852-5-8

Cover and Interior Design by Jessica Tilles/TWA Solutions

All stories appear courtesy of the author and interviewees, unless otherwise noted, and are protected under U.S. Copyright Laws.

Scriptures used are taken from the New King James Version.

"Fear not, for I am with you;
Be not dismayed, for I am your God.
I will strengthen you,
Yes, I will help you,
I will uphold you with my righteous right hand."

—Isaiah 41:10

Contents

Foreword ix
Introduction 1

Ms. Vivica... 13
3 A.M.

Eric Ross 51
The Missing Part

Anonymous 65
Off Campus

Trisha Mann-Grant.. 85
Unwanted Passenger

Shan Fiske 99
Change

Anonymous 111
The Little Girl

Your Story 119

Acknowledgements 125

Foreword

In a society filled with reality television for entertainment, *Valor 2 Victory* invites you into the lives of everyday people like you and me, and the experiences they have overcome.

Vivica Keyes leads a group of courageous individuals who found themselves in the middle of a traumatic experience and not only survived, but are continuing to live their lives and now candidly share their stories. The feelings of fear, vulnerability, and lack of sleep are real byproducts of these life-altering events. I remember Vivica sharing with me what happened to her, but it wasn't until I read her full story that I clearly realized the depth of her experience in the trials she had to overcome.

If you're like me, you'll be drawn into each story and feel the emotions of these courageous authors and their families. In a few instances, without even realizing it, I audibly responded to intense and hopeful moments of these stories.

Valor 2 Victory will spark in you a revived awareness and empathy of what is happening to people all around you and what can practically be done to assist someone in trauma. If you have an untold story, this may be your first step in removing the drama from your trauma.

— Pastor Kenneth Mulkey
Author of *Run To Win*

Introduction

I wish I did not have knowledge of any of the stories in this book.
I wish I could say they were all fiction.
I wish none of these events had occurred.
I wish my story was not a part of this book.

Valor 2 Victory
Removing the Drama from Your Trauma
7 Courageous People
7 Traumatic Experiences
7 Survivors

Valor is described as *great courage in the face of danger, especially in battle*.

Victory is described as *success in defeating an opponent or enemy*.

Something **traumatic** is described as *disturbing, shocking, distressing, damaging, agonizing, or devastating*.

This book chronicles the lives of real people who have, or are having, a *Valor 2 Victory* experience. We have been a victim of a crime or traumatic experience. We endeavor to share our stories in hopes of shedding light on what I think has been hidden in the dark for far too long.

I am not a psychiatrist, psychologist, or a clinical social worker. I am a survivor! I believe that word has been so grossly misused that we overlook the people it actually defines. We typically think of loved ones left behind when someone passes as survivors, and they are, but that is not the definition in its totality.

If you were to look up the definition, you would find that a survivor is a *person who survives, especially a person remaining alive after an event in which others have died.*

Many times, I have said a survivor is someone who had gone through a traumatic, life-threatening experience and did not die. Apparently, my thought process is accurate.

I really am a survivor! I lived!

I can appreciate, and am grateful for, all the licensed therapists that help us through these experiences. However, *Valor 2 Victory* is from perspective of the victims. I want you to hear what happened, what we felt, what we thought, and what you could have done to help us.

I will share my own experience, along with five other courageous people, who have been selfless enough to revisit that place of distress in hopes of helping someone and maybe even save a few lives and/or relationships. I know it states at the beginning there are seven stories, but I promise if you keep reading it will make sense.

Dr. Martin Luther King, Jr., put it this way. "We must build dikes of courage to hold back the flood of fear."

Introduction

We will first give you a very detailed, heartfelt, and emotional account of how a traumatic experience impacted our lives. Each person answered three specific questions:

1. What did someone/people do that really helped you?
2. What did someone/people do that really disappointed you?
3. What could someone/people have done that would have helped you?

I pray you read each story with an open heart and a willingness to be teachable. Every person is different and every person has a different kind of need, but we all have needs. After having read story after story, I am sure you will feel better armed with knowledge should you ever find yourself in the position to be that person that someone needs, God forbid.

May you never again say, "I didn't know what to do." I am confident you will find answers to that statement from one or more of our stories.

Let's unpack those three questions a bit. I will attempt to give you a glimpse into the thought process of someone who has just experienced a trauma. Remember, this is not a clinical study, but real people, with real feelings, sharing real emotions.

1. **What did someone/people do that really helped you?**
I want to applaud anyone who has ever stood by a loved one or a friend during a crisis. Having a friend who is undaunted by circumstances is invaluable. It is a very, very sensitive time for the

victim. You will need to exercise extreme caution when you decide to approach that person. If they are still in fear mode, they may feel defensive and inadvertently respond to you in a negative way. Please do not take it personally, and please do not let it detour your desire to be there to assist. Take a step back and let them express their anger or fear. It is usually a loss of control they are feeling. When you approach them with "suggestions," it can feel like you are disregarding their ability to make sound decisions. You may be right, but remember this is not about you. Do not become confrontational. This person has just been in a situation where they were taken advantage of and they have a real need to regain control. It's not personal! Just breathe and listen patiently to your loved one. It is not uncommon for them to shout and tell you that you are trying to control them in one breath and then be in tears in the next. Their emotions may be out of control. They may have serious trust issues. If you could imagine someone going through puberty, PMS, menopause, midlife crisis, and dementia all at the same time, then you would better understand their vulnerability.

> They are pondering:
> Am I safe?
> Can I trust this person?
> Do they have my best interest at heart?

> At the same time, wondering:
> Why is this person trying to tell me how I feel?

Introduction

Why are they not listening to me?
Why are they trying to control me?

And, at the same time, thinking:
Why are they asking me so many questions?
Why are they telling me they know how I feel?
Are they concerned or just nosy (prying)?

One of the main things you can do at this time is to be patient. Don't give up. They really do need you.

2. **What did someone/people do that disappointed you?**

This one may surprise you. There are people that you would have bet a million dollars would have been in your corner in a crisis that will not even call. That can be heartbreaking. It can really add to the stress of the trauma when the victim is measuring everything and everyone. In their despair, there is an expectation of family and friends coming to the rescue. When that fails, it can add to their sense of vulnerability. There's that word again—vulnerability. It will probably be repeated a few times because there is no other word that quite captures this situation. Just so we are clear, vulnerable means *capable of or susceptible to being wounded or hurt; as by a weapon; open to moral attack, criticism, open to assault, difficult to defend*

Wow! This says that the person feels the type of pain that one feels when a weapon is involved. In other words, if someone had been cut or shot, their wounds would be visible and they would receive immediate medical attention. The wound referenced in this text is internal and though it cannot be seen, it requires the same urgency and attention.

It says they feel defenseless. Your words, actions, and deeds toward this person, at that specific time, are being measured. They hear and respond to *exactly* what you say and respond accordingly. Please do not make them have to defend themselves against you by trying to explain how they feel or having to apologize for hurting your feelings. They are wounded and trying to make sense out of something that most likely makes no sense.

I want to ask you a tough question. If you receive a call that this person has been killed, how would you respond? That is the same way you need to respond when they live! Instead of taking flowers and burning candles when they die, take flowers and burn candles when they did not die. They are mourning. They lost their sense of security. Respond as if you are visiting a grieving friend, because that is precisely what they are in that moment.

Contacting them after the initial incident and then disappearing is confusing because now they know that you know, and you're not there. There is a sense of abandonment. They question the relationship and sometimes rightfully so. It is during these times that relationships may be defined. Are you my friend or just an acquaintance? Did you ever really love me or care about me or was it all a façade? Be very careful during these times. The damage can sometimes be irreparable. Even if you remain *friends* you could be placed in a different category in the heart of the victim. "I'm sorry" helps, but cannot immediately

Introduction

mend the disappointment. You can also become their hero by exceeding their expectations. It is a pleasant surprise when someone unexpectedly offers comfort and support. Be consistent. Be gentle. Be available.

3. **What could someone/people have done that would have helped you?**

I have one answer for that: JUST SHOW UP.

In regards to trauma, these are the most powerful three words anyone could ever share with you:

JUST SHOW UP!

What does that mean? It means just that, JUST SHOW UP. I cannot emphasize that enough. This person is not capable of delegating duties. They are probably not concerned with mundane tasks. They don't care if the dishes are still in the sink or if they made their bed. They are trying to survive. If you JUST SHOW UP, you can see the dishes in the sink or the unmade bed and handle that for them. Those are necessary but not a priority. Can you imagine someone calling and asking if you would be willing to come to their home and load the dishwasher? You would think they had gone off the deep end. Chances are, they will not ask, but it needs to be done. Be the initiator. JUST SHOW UP and look around; you will see it when you arrive.

Most people call, listen, and then say, "Call me if you need anything." Albeit well intentioned, do you really mean it? What if the person would like you to go with them to the grocery store tomorrow? You are not available tomorrow. So now the traumatized victim is rejected. They feel like a burden. Let me tell you what they are not going to do: call three more people to possibly get the same response.

When you call, be precise. "I am available Wednesday and would like to know if there is anything I can do at that time." You might also say, "I'm on my way over right now. Can I bring you anything?"

You will most likely find very little resistance from the victim. In fact, you have just helped them tremendously. You have made a decision that did not require their input. That is huge! They have probably been bombarded with decisions, especially if law enforcement is involved. They are asked a million questions in the immediate aftermath and for some time into the future.

Your friend may have spent a lot of time creating a garden and in that season, every one of those plants, flowers, and/or trees is disposable. JUST SHOW UP. Water the garden. I assure you, your friend will thank you. It may be a few weeks or even months later, but when the fog lifts and they see the garden flourishing, they will be so very grateful. Every little thing helps.

Were they in the middle of laundry? Are the clothes still in the washer? A whole load of clothes that have been in the washer so long they have mildewed could be only worthy of a plastic bag to be discarded, but a friend would rewash the clothes and put them in the dryer. JUST SHOW UP.

Another thing before we move on. Be very careful in your choice of words. If you ask, "How are you?" and they answer, "Terrified," how are you going to respond? Are you prepared to

Introduction

drop everything and get to them quickly? If not, do not ask that question! You will only make them more despondent.

You may simply want to say, "I was thinking about you" or "Would you like to talk?"

You may want to review the details so you call and have a long conversation, and then, after all the horrid information, you say "Okay, I'll call you later." You just took them back to the center of the trauma and dropped them off. Now you've abandoned them for the comfort and safety of your world. Never end a conversation with them discussing the incident. Try to talk about something else prior to hanging up.

One last thing (until I think of another thing), do not say, "I am going to pray *for* you" without praying *with* them right then. Reassure them that you will continue to do so beyond that conversation.

Be mindful of your loved one's activity. Are they staying in the house? Are they afraid to go home? Are they eating? They may not know how or even recognize this change. They will cling to what makes them feel safer while completely overlooking their normal behavior. They will not see it. That's where you come in, *friend!* Help them navigate their way back. That might just mean dropping by their home and sitting with them. You could be reading or quietly watching a movie. Your company could be all they need. It's not always about your having to resolve the issue. It's more of you JUST SHOWING UP.

The person you love is still in there. We can't leave them stuck. We can't let their lives be a pretense. We can't have tears behind the smiles. We can't pretend we don't see it.

We have to give them a voice. They just want to be heard. This horrible, horrific, devastating injustice really did happen. They *were* a victim. They are *now* victorious. They *survived*.

Our goal is to create a pathway for this courageous person, who has faced danger and/or been in a battle, to become successful in defeating their jolting and scarring opponent or enemy.

With faith, hope, and good people willing to listen, care for and show up, our loved ones will recover completely. They will then be able to help others just as the people in the book.

The seventh chapter of this book was left blank intentionally just for you. We encourage you to write your story or the story of someone you know, with their permission, of course. It can be healing and cathartic.

Valor 2 Victory is a series that will continue to share stories of triumph. Stories when ordinary people under extraordinary circumstances become valiant role models.

If you would like to submit your story for publication consideration, we would love to hear from you.

Please send a short detailed account, along with your contact information, to MsVivica@prazeup.com.

For His Glory,
Ms. Vivica

"You may never know what results come from your action, but if you do nothing there will be no result."

—Mahatma Gandhi

3 A.M.

The week of January 19, 2014 started off a little busier than most. It was our annual kick-off time with one of the companies I represent in the insurance industry. That meant meeting after meeting after meeting to discuss the projections for the new year. As a manager, there were additional meetings to strategize our game plan for our teams. Some of the South Carolina home office team had flown in for the week as well. Our Territory Kick-Off meeting was in full gear.

On Wednesday, January 22, 2014, I invited one of the ladies from our home office to dinner. It had been a long day. I arrived home late, tired, and full from a good meal. Remembering Thursday was street cleaning day on my street, I decided to pull my SUV into the driveway so I wouldn't have to get up early the next morning to move it before leaving for work. Finally, I was in the house. I took a shower and put on my pajamas. I read some, watched television and then went to bed.

On January 23rd, at approximately 3:00 A.M., I heard an extremely loud crashing sound with glass splattering. I jumped out of my bed and looked out of the window to see a small light-colored pickup truck (with a metal tool box in rear) making a three-point turn and speeding off. I assumed he had just hit a parked car and was fleeing. I stared at it for a while, trying to see if I could get the license plate information or any other specifics. I wanted to be able to give the details to whichever neighbor owned the presumed car. I was glad I had moved my SUV off the street before going to bed, since this was clearly a hit and run, or so I thought.

Awakened and shaken, I went into the kitchen, which is at the front of the house. As I was about to turn on the light, the running water caught my attention. The faucet was running full force. Perplexed, I went to the sink and turned it off. Then I noticed the blinds at the window over the kitchen sink appeared to be sticking out away from the window. Raising the blinds, I discovered my window had been broken. I saw red liquid all over my counter. Because everything was silent, my first thought was that someone from that fleeing car had thrown something through my window. I couldn't imagine why, but that's the only thing I could surmise. I grabbed my landline phone, realizing I would now need to call the sheriff. I was frustrated because I knew I would be up all night. First waiting on the sheriff to respond to this non-emergency call and then getting someone at this time of the morning to repair a broken window. I went back to the bedroom to get my robe. My home alarm started to sound. Now very confused as to what had triggered it, I returned to the entry way to disarm it. I assumed it was a delayed reaction from the broken window. To this day, I still do not know what triggered that alarm. The house was in 'stay' mode so motion would not have done it. I returned to the kitchen, turned on the light, and

3 A.M.

noticed red liquid strewn over the counter and on the floor. I started looking under the counter, the table and all through the kitchen for some type of container, which someone could have thrown through my window full of this red liquid. I could not find anything. Even more bizarre, at first glance, this red liquid appeared to be only in the kitchen. The floor was clean for about the next three feet. As I looked further, I noticed the trail resumed in the dining room. What could have rolled into there? I thought. I stepped into the dining room, still nothing. Then I entered the living room and to my utter shock, horror, and dismay, there was a man! He was standing there, silent, in the dark, covered in blood.

There are no words to describe what I thought or felt. I screamed! I screamed continuously. I screamed as loud and long as I could. This was a scream that I had never heard from myself before. My own screams added to my fear.

He lunged toward me and grabbed me. My fear was indescribable. I was alone in my home and not sure if anyone heard my screams. He may have grunted, but did not say any audible words. We tussled. I fought back with all my might. He was trying to grab me around my shoulders or around my neck. I was trying not to let him get a good grip. I am not sure of how long this went on, but it seemed like an eternity. At some point, everything stopped. He just stood there. I heard a voice say, "He's not fighting anymore. Stop." I believe it was the voice of the Holy Spirit. I realized that was my moment to get away. I began to back away. He was positioned with his back to the kitchen and the front entry way. My back was to the family room. I realized

Ms. Vivica

I was still holding my phone. I tried to dial 911. I was yelling for him to get out. I misdialed and heard a recording coming from the handset. I was trying not to look down at the phone in case he came toward me again. He just stood there looking dazed. He appeared to be intoxicated or high on something. He stared at the ceiling, then his bleeding arms, then around the room. I redialed 911. I continued to walk backward and ease into the family room, still yelling for him to get out. The 911 operator answered and I screamed that someone was in my house, that he had attacked me and that he was bleeding profusely all over the place. She was asking me all sorts of questions and I was trying to answer. It was so chaotic. I had to get out of the house. I looked at my newly installed plantation shutters in the family room on the sliding doors. I remember hearing the installer's voice in my head, telling me that all the shutters needed to be properly closed for the doors to slide open. I ran my hands across them quickly. I did not want anything impeding my escape.

    I managed to get the sliding door to my patio open and I ran out of the house. I ran faster than I have ever run in my life. I didn't know if he was following me. I did not look back. I ran to a neighbor's house directly across the street. I was talking to the 911 operator the entire time. She was trying to calm me down to get details. I was frantic. Thank God I was using a landline. My address could be seen immediately. I made it across the street. I banged on my neighbor's door and rang the doorbell. I was still screaming that someone was in my house. He answered and could barely make out what I was saying. His security door was locked

3 A.M.

and he was trying to get the keys. That was the first time I looked behind me to see if I had been followed. I had not. He opened the door and stepped out just as the first sheriff car was arriving. I hung up with the 911 dispatcher. I went to the female deputy and gave her the details and stated that he was still in my house. She asked me to stay back. Another car arrived and she wanted to know if there was an alley behind my house or a shared wall with another house. I responded that it was another house. She instructed the second sheriff car to go to the next street. More sheriff cars were arriving. They asked me how they could make entry and I let them know that the sliding door was open on the patio that I had just escaped from. They instructed me to stay at my neighbors. My neighbor offered me a pair of shoes to put on since I was barefoot. I was trying to regain my composure. I was inside when my neighbor's girlfriend, Beatrice, said, "They got him, they're bringing him out." I stepped outside. I saw this young, white man lying on the ground in handcuffs, with several deputies asking him questions.

I couldn't really see him from that distance. I asked one of the deputies if I could get a closer look. I explained that I had just had a lot of work done on my home and wanted to see if this was someone that may have been with one of the contractors. I stepped just close enough to know that I had never seen him before. They put him on a gurney, handcuffed, and into the back of an ambulance. The female deputy remained and asked several questions and took pictures of the crime scene; at least that's what I thought it was. As she was finishing her photo shoot, she had not taken one picture of me. Beatrice said, "There's blood all over her. Aren't you going to take her picture?" The deputy looked at me and said, "Oh yeah. Lift your arms up." *Click, click.* "Turn around." *Click.*

I complied. She never asked me if any of the blood was mine. In fact, not one of the emergency responders asked me if I was hurt or if I needed medical attention. I was still in shock at that time and didn't even know there was blood on me. Everyone left. Only my neighbors and I remained.

That part of my nightmare was over and another one was just beginning.

We went inside to assess the damage. There was blood everywhere. The kitchen counter was besieged in glass and blood. There was a trail across the kitchen floor. The side of the off-white sofa was drenched on one corner and the pillows had been splattered with blood. The rugs, walls, and dining room chairs had all been impacted. There was a pool of blood with skid marks on the hardwood floors in the living room where the altercation had occurred. It was everywhere.

I just kept repeating, "Look at all this blood!" My neighbor, William, told me to walk away. He said for me not to look at it. He asked for something to clean with. I don't remember what I gave him. I went into the bathroom and looked at myself in the mirror. Blood was covering my shoulders and arms. I took off my robe, threw it in the bathtub and turned on the water. I needed to get out of the pajamas next, and quickly. I went into the bedroom and changed clothes. I gathered everything from the bedroom and bathroom, went to the garage, and put the soiled items in the

3 A.M.

washing machine. I felt like I couldn't get it off me. I wanted to take a shower, but there was so much damage in my house that I decided to clean everything first. Otherwise, I would contaminate even more areas of my home. I returned to the living room with fabric cleaner and started frantically spraying the sofa, rugs and anything in my range.

About ten to fifteen minutes had passed. There was a knock at the door. It was two of the deputies returning to inform me they had spoken with this bloody boogie man from the dark. The female deputy did the talking. She said his story was that he had been in the pickup truck I had seen earlier and he "got spooked" and jumped out of the truck because he thought they were going to harm him. I asked her, "How did he know that I would not harm him?" She said he chose to take his chances with what he would find in my house than to stay in that truck. She also said she was inclined to believe him because she had located the truck. She said she had gone to the street where he said he had been and found the truck based on my description. She approached and touched the hood and the engine was still warm. Inside the truck she found one of his shoes and his cell phone. The cell phone had a text message that someone was going to harm him. She claimed she also spoke with the owner of the truck. She indicated she didn't think he really wanted to hurt me because he was just trying to get away. She said this in a, you-know-what-I-mean kind of tone.

I asked her how he would be charged. I asked if this was considered a burglary.

Ms. Vivica

She said, "No, he didn't steal anything."

"Is it breaking and entering since it was forced entry?" I asked, and she implied he was somehow justified because he was afraid. I then asked if the fact that he attacked me constituted assault. I said, "He grabbed me!"

She shrugged and said, "Yeah, but you're not hurt."

My whole demeanor changed. She left. Something did not feel right. I told my neighbor to stop cleaning and I went to get my camera and took pictures. Although we had cleaned quite a bit at that point, there was still enough to indicate that something had occurred. After I took pictures we continued cleaning.

Another ten to fifteen minutes passed. I had gone into the bedroom for something and heard communication coming from what sounded like a police scanner. I looked out the window and saw two sheriff cars in front of my house, *again*. The female deputy was standing at the rear of her vehicle talking to two people in plain clothes. I assumed that maybe they were detectives. I stepped outside. She approached me to tell me that they were his family members and that they would like to talk to me. I was shocked. His family members! I agreed to speak with them. I wanted to know who they were because they now knew who I was and where I lived. She introduced them as his parents. They apologized and told me that their son had never been arrested. They wanted to convince me not to press charges. I asked if he had been in trouble before and they said no. I asked them if he had a drinking or drug problem and that's when I received a different response. After hesitating, and some thought, his mother

3 A.M.

stated she did not know. I immediately recognized that as a sign of trying to answer a question, and tell the truth, but not reveal any information. In my mind, she probably asked herself if she had ever seen him use drugs. We all know that is not the same as seeing him after the fact when you can only guess what he drank, smoked, or shot up. This was a mother's I-want-to-protect-my-son kind of response. This was also the only time the father did not respond at all.

They began to plead with me not to press charges.

"Will you look at what your son did?" I shouted, pointing inside the house. At this point, I was irate. I couldn't believe they were asking me not to press charges after what their son had done to my home, without assessing the damage because it was more than a broken window. Reluctantly, they looked inside.

Although we had been cleaning, the scene was still horrific.

His mother gasped when she saw the blood. I could not imagine what was going through her mind, witnessing a scene filled with that much blood, knowing it came from her son. I do not recall if they asked me if I had been injured. They were more concerned with their son not getting a criminal record.

"We will pay for the damages," they said.

"That's not my primary concern," I told them. "I want to get all your son's blood out of my house."

Again, she asked me not to press charges.

"I won't make any decisions tonight," I told her. I was in no condition to do so. "I'll pray about it," I said, and then I asked for their names and contact information. Since they had my information, I at least wanted to know who I was talking to. I had also planned to do an Internet search to see what I could find out about them.

The deputy asked me to sign a form that she described as an arrest form. I am not sure if she referred to this as a citizen's arrest. I would normally have paid closer attention, but I was traumatized and still under the impression that I was the victim. I assumed she was looking out for my best interest.

Anna, my cousin, arrived while this conversation was taking place. This was the first time, I believe, I actually took a real breath.

After my neighbor, William, and I had cleaned as much as we could, he stayed with us a while. Once he left, I recounted the events of the morning to Anna.

I had located an emergency window repair company and scheduled an appointment. I was waiting a bit to contact my carpet and upholstery cleaner since it was still before sunrise.

It was then, sitting on the sofa, that I scratched my head. The back of my hair was hard. I turned to Anna and asked, "What do you see?" She told me to remove my hands and told me that my hair was matted down. I was horrified. Was I bleeding and didn't know it? Had I been injured? How could my home, only moments earlier, have been filled with first responders and no one noticed? Anna looked carefully and we concluded it was not my blood but that of my assailant. Oh my goodness. His blood was not just all over my house and my clothes, but in my hair, too. I wanted to scream again. My mind was racing. Was that drugged out person contaminated? I had hoped not. I was grateful I did

3 A.M.

not have any open wounds. I couldn't touch it. I would need to contact my stylist immediately. I had just been in the salon two days prior, but I would go back as soon as she opened and have her not only wash, but disinfect my hair and scalp. One more thing I needed to do. I felt sick.

My mind was full of questions. I wondered who this family was that would receive a call in the middle of the night and be allowed to come to the victim's home—my home. I needed to know more.

I decided to call the number they had given me. I was a little curious. Was it even the right number? It was. His mother answered. I identified myself. I reiterated that it might not be a good idea for them to try to pay for all the damages since I had just received an estimate of $200 just to board the window. She said that was fine. I told her I would think about it and let her know. I asked about her son. She stated they had gone home after they left my house and had not seen him. She thought he was in LB Memorial or maybe Lakewood Regional, but not sure. I found that interesting since they found me within one hour of the incident. At least another hour or two had passed and she did not know the whereabouts of their son.

Now my brain was starting to function. I was becoming increasingly suspicious. How did they find me so quickly, especially since it was my understanding their son was not a minor? Who had called them?

I decided to call my homeowners insurance company. They wanted to send an adjuster to meet me. He would arrive Friday afternoon to assess the damage.

Ms. Vivica

I had the carpet and upholstery cleaned that morning. Because I had used his service many times in the past, Mr. Petersen rearranged his day to fit me in. I was grateful. But, even after having everything cleaned, I wasn't sure what it would look like once it dried or how safe it would be.

I went to the salon. I sent my stylist, Jamika Wilson, a text to briefly tell her what happened. I asked her not to mention it. However, when I walked in, she started tearing up and a few other stylists hugged me. They were so concerned and compassionate. I warned the young lady that was to wash my hair to be careful and to wear gloves since my hair was filled with blood. She did. She told me the bowl turned red as she let the water run through my hair.

The rest of the day was filled with contacting the necessary people. I did not tell very many people everything. The few people I told, although it was because of their concern, wanted to ask me about the details over and over. I could not talk about it anymore. I could not keep reliving it. It was still too fresh. So I decided not to share it any further, for the moment.

I went home to take care of all the business that still needed to be handled. Every light in the house was on. I thought I would be okay. I was wrong. The later it got, the more terrified I became. I sat paralyzed in my bedroom. I was afraid to leave the room. Everything that could be used as a weapon surrounded me. I heard everything. I was listening so intently I could distinguish the crickets from the spiders. I was on guard. I didn't even want to go to sleep. At some point, I simply passed out.

3 A.M.

I missed the meetings and events on Thursday for my job. Friday morning around 9:00 A.M., I was awakened by the phone ringing. It was a colleague asking if I was planning to attend the managers meeting that morning. I asked, "What meeting?" He reminded me our legal team from the home office wanted to share information with us. I told him I would be there as soon as I could. I jumped up and got ready as quickly as possible. I felt like a zombie. It had been about thirty hours since the incident and I only slept about two of those hours. I rushed to the office. My phone was ringing off the hook. I'm not even sure who I was talking to. I was exhausted.

I felt an overwhelming sense of abandonment, like I was not safe. I had never experienced anything like that before. I was scared, angry and vulnerable. I wondered why God had allowed this to happen to me. Being the only woman on the street who lives alone, if he had gone in any other house, he would have encountered a man or multiple people. A man could have defended himself and protected his family. Then, I felt guilty for having those thoughts. I couldn't wish that upon my neighbors. They would not deserve anything like this to happen to them. So then I became burdened with questions of why this happened at all. I believe God has to allow all things in my life, so what was the purpose of this? What was this fear supposed to teach me? How long would I feel this? All I could do was keep praying, *Help me, Jesus.*

Just as I was about to pull into the underground parking at the office the phone rang again. I answered it.

Ms. Vivica

"Hello," I said, sounding frustrated.

There was a soft voice on the other end. "May I speak to Ms. Vivica, please?"

"This is she."

"Good morning. This is Elder Dora from Church One in Long Beach."

"Who is this?"

"Elder Dora from Church One."

I had no idea who it was. "How can I help you?"

"I attended your Children's Ministry Leaders Conference a couple years ago and I was praying about whom to ask to be a guest speaker for us this year for our Children's Appreciation Day, and the Lord put you on my heart. It's not until June, but I wanted to know if you would consider it and I wanted to give you time to pray about it."

I was so confused. Five minutes before that call I was trying to figure where God was and… now I was broken. Those simple words, "God put you on my heart," had ministered to me. I could hear God telling me, "I see you."

I explained that I was about to pull into an underground garage and lose my signal. I asked Elder Dora to please call me right back and leave all her information in my voicemail and I promised to call her back.

I took my parking ticket and followed the arrows down to the parking area for my office. I backed my car in a space and turned off the ignition. I dropped my head on the steering wheel and, for the first time, I cried. God did see me. He had put me on the

3 A.M.

heart of someone to reach out to me at that exact moment. He couldn't let the despair I was feeling include Him. He couldn't let another second go without letting me know He was there. He was the reason I survived. He was the reason I was not raped, badly beaten, or killed. He was there all the time. I knew that no matter how difficult it would become, He was going to see me through.

I dried my eyes, got out the car, and took the elevator to the office. I stopped in the ladies room to check my appearance. I looked tired. My eyes were still a little red, but I had to go in. I asked the Territory Manager and someone from home office that I knew well if I could speak with them privately. We went into his office. I told them everything that happened. I did not attend the meeting the day before and now I was late for this meeting, so I reluctantly told them about it. I had never been so irresponsible as to not show up or call for a meeting. They understood and told me if I needed to leave they would understand. It was so hard to keep telling people.

The insurance adjuster met me when I returned home. He stated they would need to send in a hazardous materials unit in to clean every area that had been exposed to blood. However, that would not be possible until Monday morning. They suggested I stay at a hotel until that time. That was just fine with me.

That evening was to be our semi-formal, black tie awards gala. I had invited a guest who was to receive an award for all his support the prior year, ironically a law enforcement official and good friend. I felt compelled to attend and I did. I did not tell anyone what had happened.

Ms. Vivica

Prior to the event, at approximately 4:30 P.M., I contacted Lakewood Sheriff Station to ask if I could get the name of the detective assigned to my case and the report number.

My call was answered by a deputy or a Law Enforcement Tech (LET). I told her the reason for my call. She asked for my name. I gave it to her. She asked for my address. I gave it to her. She put me on hold. She returned. She asked me for the name of my street again. I repeated it. She put me on hold. She returned and asked if this was possibly a domestic violence incident. I said no. She put me on hold, again. She returned and asked if this involved a neighbor. I said no, and before she could put me on hold again I stopped her and asked, "Are you trying to tell me that there is no report?" She said, "No, ma'am, there is no report."

She transferred me to the Watch Deputy. He told me the incident report stated an agreement had been made between me and the parents with them agreeing to pay for damages and no further action was required. I told him I had made no such agreement. I was appalled. He asked me several questions, including if I knew the criminal, accept he called out his name. That was the first time I had heard his name. He then told me to call back after 10:00 P.M. that night when the first responding female deputy would be on duty. He said she normally worked in Hawaiian Gardens, but he would let her return to take my report. Why would I want to talk to the same deputy who had been here originally, seen everything, brought the parents to my house, and didn't even think she needed to write it down? I was livid. Not to mention he thought it could wait six more hours.

3 A.M.

That was the first opportunity the sheriff had to correct this. He could have sent a car to me right then to take an accurate report. He chose not to.

I called right back and asked for someone in operations. My call was routed back to him. Without identifying myself this time I asked to be connected to someone in operations. I was transferred to a voicemail and I left a message. Knowing it was approaching 5:00 P.M. on a Friday, I was not surprised.

I thought this would be a simple call to obtain the information I requested and I would be able to get on with my evening plans. Nothing was making sense. I was agitated and filled with anxiety all over again.

I had to get ready for the awards gala. I wanted to be there to support my team for all their hard work in 2013. I would handle the sheriff the next day.

I put on my new dress and shoes. I put on a little more makeup than usual, trying to camouflage the circles that had formed under my eyes from lack of sleep. I put on my happy manager's face and went to the affair. I wore my façade of a smile all evening. When I returned home I took off that dress and laid it neatly on my bed. I put on a yoga/workout suit. I grabbed an overnight bag and filled it with my pajamas and toiletries. As suggested by the homeowner's insurance company, Wawanesa, I made a reservation at a nearby hotel. I could not go another night in that condition. I left my home and checked into the Cerritos Sheraton. I was finally able to do the one thing that had eluded me, sleep.

Saturday, January 25th at approximately 1:20 P.M., I arrived at Lakewood Station to request a copy of this incident report

Ms. Vivica

that was supposed to indicate an agreement between me and the criminal's parents. I spoke with a law enforcement tech at the counter. She first indicated I needed to go to the office in Artesia to get a copy and repeatedly said there was no report. She was talking pretty loud, but not looking at me. She was talking above my head and into the open air. It was strange. I told her I was not aware of any office in Artesia and requested an address. She left the counter and was gone for quite some time. She returned and said they wanted me to go home. I asked who wanted me to go home. She kept repeating herself. I was to go home and a deputy would be sent from my area to take my report. I asked her who gave this instruction. She finally stated it was the Watch Commander.

I returned home. At approximately 2:45 P.M., a deputy arrived. I asked her why she was there. I did not trust them or this process anymore. After a few questions and watching her response, I realized she was not quite sure what was going on. Whatever was happening, she didn't appear to be a part of it. I invited her in to take the report.

Just as I let her in, I received a call from someone at the station to let me know a deputy was dispatched and was on the way. I let him know she had arrived. This was the second opportunity for them to correct their error.

I was finally given a report number and provided information for victims. I was still concerned since the deputy listed it as vandalism and assault. That still seemed to be a bit soft. I always thought the deputies were to include everything in the initial

3 A.M.

report and leave it up to the detectives to sort it out. I felt the report should have included something indicating forced entry and battery. But, at least I had a report.

I returned to the hotel.

On that Monday, I met the insurance adjuster and hazardous materials company at my home. I was informed they did not clean blood, but they would remove all porous items (i.e., rugs, pillows, drywall, etc.) considered to be hazardous material. That meant I would lose all rugs, dining chairs, and the walls and floor boards would need to be cut out and replaced. I negotiated with him to have the sofa reupholstered versus destroyed. It had sentimental value since it is a custom piece I designed. My robe, paper towel holder, and several other items that came in contact with the blood would be discarded. I would have to stay in a hotel until the process was completed. It was estimated that it would be about two weeks. I packed another bag.

On January 28, 2014, I called Internal Affairs. There is a 1-800 phone line that allows you to record your grievance. I stated everything that transpired.

February 7, 11:45 A.M.

I was contacted by a sergeant and asked about the specifics of my complaint. I gave him the details. He stated the responding deputy had done a good job. I am still trying to figure out what he meant. What was the good part? Was it the dismissal of the facts, bringing the parents to my home, the failure to file a report or the overall neglect?

Ms. Vivica

During the conversation, he told me a Suspicious Circumstances Report was filed by the female deputy who was the first to arrive on the night of the incident. He also told me that since that time they had contacted the suspect, and was informed he was not afraid, but drunk. He had no recollection of that night. I asked how this changed the sheriff's position since their original response was based solely on him being afraid. No comment. And, what about that text message the deputy claims to have seen? No comment.

He said he would like me to meet with the detectives to discuss conflict resolution. I was appalled. What was there to discuss? I told him I was totally dissatisfied with how the department was handling the matter and that I was going to seek legal counsel.

More than once it was stated to me that they needed to make sure the young man was okay. What the heck?

Who was this criminal or his family that everyone was trying to protect?

How do you respond to that type of attitude? The only way to describe this is if you are an African American watching a movie about slavery and the slave describes some injustice to the slave master and is told to quit complaining because you cannot tell anything on a white man. Whatever he did was considered legal because you have no rights. You are not considered equal. You are not even considered a person. You cringe. You think, *I could have never made it 'back then'*. Well, this was today and I was experiencing racism in such a way I would have never imagined. I didn't know what to do with this emotion. Prejudice!! That does

3 A.M.

not fit in my life or in my heart. It certainly does not fit with the God I serve and believe in whole-heartedly.

I had never experienced this before. I grew up in Los Angeles, California, and then moved to an integrated but predominantly white neighborhood, Lynwood, California. I never felt slighted. I never felt inferior. I have worked in corporate America where at times there were very few people of color. I am not naïve enough to say it was never present, but I am saying it was never blatant. It never impacted my life. I have never let it alter any decision in my life. I am still grasping to find some other explanation for this behavior. To date, nothing has surfaced.

I was referred to a detective who reiterated the sentiments of the sergeant. He went on to state that everything had been done in a timely matter and since all the suspect did was "place his hands" on my shoulders, there was no need for assault or battery charges. I was screaming and pleading and crying, once again, that this man was not a guest in my home and this had not been a waltz! He broke in and attacked me. His patronizing response indicated, in his opinion that I was overreacting.

February 10th

I spoke with a lady at the Ombudsmen office. She suggested I have a conversation with the detectives to pursue the case being presented to the district attorney's office. I was to contact her office when I received the response letter from Internal Affairs. I told her I was going to request a meeting with the station captain.

I spoke with the captain's secretary and requested a meeting with the captain.

Ms. Vivica

February 11th

I was told I would not be able to meet with the captain, but I should speak with detectives.

February 12th

A detective contacted me and asked me to repeat this horrific encounter once again. As I was repeating what happened, he had a few statements and comments that were particularly interesting to me. He said the suspect had remained in the hospital for a couple of days and they wanted to make sure he was not hurt. My response was that I did not want him to die, but the only reason he was hurt was because he forced himself through my double-paned glass window. He also stated the female deputy had done a good job by handling this on the first night. I informed him she had not displayed any concern for my well-being. I had blood on my robe and the back of my head. She never suggested that maybe the paramedics should examine me to make sure I had not been injured. I wanted to know if bringing the parents of an adult suspect to the victim's home without consent was doing a good job. He had no reply. He wanted to know when the suspect "placed his hands on my shoulders" if I had punched him.

First of all, I was offended at the use of the phrase, "placed his hands on my shoulders." He grabbed me! I was screaming at the top of my lungs and he lunged toward me and grabbed me. This was not a dance. I was fighting to defend myself and save my life. Isn't it interesting that he used *placed* for the intruder and *punched* for me.

I digress.

3 A.M.

He asked me to define grab. I could not believe this. He wanted to know how long he held me. I told him it felt like a lifetime, but at that moment I did not time it since freeing myself from his grasp was more important to me. He told me these were the type of questions a district attorney would ask. I let him know my response would be the same. I asked him if he wanted me to make something up since the truth didn't seem to satisfy him. He said, "No." I felt as if he were trying to minimize the events from that night. I told him I had served the L.A. County Sheriff for the last ten years in the capacity of an insurance agent and had visited them in hospitals, attended retirement and birthday parties, and donated money when one of them was in need. At that very moment, my business card was hanging in their station for them to contact me if they needed help. He did acknowledge he may have known who I was. I told him I was beyond disappointed; now that I needed them they had let me down. This conversation was just one day shy of two weeks and this was my first conversation with a detective. He let me know he would be busy the next day and I would hear from him on Friday. I did not receive a call on Friday.

On Tuesday, February 18, 2014, I received that call from the detective. He informed me that the Los Angeles County District Attorney's office had agreed to file charges. The suspect would be allowed to enter a plea at his arraignment on March 10, 2014. The detective told me I did not need to attend this arraignment. When I asked him what charges had been filed, he was vague. He said there would be multiple charges.

Ms. Vivica

I knew they were not making decisions in my best interest so I called the district attorney's office. My suspensions were confirmed. Only misdemeanor trespassing and vandalism charges were filed. I was devastated. The images of the slave movie returned. They had not deemed it a crime for him to grab me without provocation or permission.

I visited the district attorney's office and asked to speak with the person assigned to my case. I requested he review the facts and to make sure the appropriate charges were being filed. I asked if he had seen the pictures of the crime scene. He was not aware of any pictures.

The case went forward as planned. On March 10, 2014, the suspect pled no contest to two misdemeanor charges: vandalism and trespassing.

On March 11, 2014, I received a letter indicating that Internal Affairs agreed with me. My claims that the Sheriff's department mishandled my case were FOUNDED! Finally, some admission of wrongdoing. Hallelujah! Not so fast… it was more like a small, yay.

I received a letter from the district attorney's office, as well as a phone call regarding restitution. I asked what was the law regarding misdemeanor versus felony charges. I was told the loss had to be over $400 for it to be considered a felony. That was the broken window alone. So how was it with over $20,000 in damages this person was only charged with a misdemeanor?

I'm sorry, I forgot…

I was not considered a person. Therefore, nothing I owned could have been of any value.

3 A.M.

On March 21, 2014, I received a call from a district attorney who stated he proceeded with the case based on the information provided by the Sheriff's department. For clarity, this was a different district attorney than the one I had spoken to previously. He said the report indicated that the suspect had only "placed his hands" on my shoulders and that did not appear to be a violent act. There were those same insulting words again. "He placed his hands…" Doesn't it sound gingerly? As if it was a tender or kind gesture. Where were my manners? At 3:00 A.M. when someone comes through your window, they should be welcomed with open arms. Perhaps I should have served tea and crumpets.

He mentioned he had a conversation with the suspect and he didn't remember the entire incident. He seemed to think that made sense and that surely I would understand. I had to stop and ask him to repeat that. He tried to make it sound like it was normal.

After all, "You can't possibly have a conversation with everyone, in every case," he said.

My response, "So, let me get this right. You mean to tell me that there were two people in the house that night and you chose to have a conversation with the criminal, burglar, assaulter, not the victim/homeowner?"

Again I say, "What the heck!" He admitted that was exactly what he had done, but had no further comment.

I attended the restitution hearing on April 24. I was accompanied by my cousin Anna, and three of my best friends, Lisa, Kim, and April. I greatly appreciate each of these women.

Ms. Vivica

They were with me through it all. We met at the courthouse that morning. I was sworn in to provide testimony, mostly about the value of the items that had been damaged or destroyed. I placed emphasis on the fact that I was repeatedly assaulted. The judge continued the case after learning there were photos of the crime scene that could potentially confirm my allegations. He demanded the photos be produced and entered into evidence. The next court day was scheduled for Friday, May 30, 2014.

I prayed further and asked God to lead me to the right lawyer. I was sure I would not be heard without legal representation. The emotional and physical drain on me was taking its toll. I had returned to work, sporadically, but I was not fully functioning. I was constantly looking over my shoulder. Loud noises and sudden moves frightened me. There were movies and TV shows I found difficult to watch. Some of them triggered painful memories. I was not myself. I was able to get dressed and comb my hair, but that was on the outside. Inside, I was deeply troubled.

On Friday May 23, 2014, I retained legal counsel. She informed me she would have some information for me after the Memorial Day weekend. And that she did.

Tuesday, May 27, 2014, I was interviewed by Channel 4 News reporter, Beverly White. She could have been given an exclusive, but passed and said not to deny additional coverage. Channel 5 News reporter, Mark Mester, was next. Both came to my home later that day for additional footage. Channel 5 broadcasted live that evening from my front yard. That was odd, to say the least. I was in the house watching it on TV.

3 A.M.

The next morning, we did a full press release with every local news channel, including Telemundo. Several radio and newspapers covered the story as well. The two facts that seem to pique their interest the most was the parents showing up and the letter from Internal Affairs stating my allegations were founded. I had no idea how rare that was.

When we returned to court on May 30, 2014, it was a whole different scenario than the one I left back in April. It was hostile. Clearly, I misunderstood the terminology "resume." I thought that meant we were going to pick up where we left off, which would have been with me on the stand being questioned by the district attorney, and ending with the judge asking for the photos. However, that is not what happened. I returned to the stand, but this time I was berated by questions from the prosecutor. Yes, the prosecutor in a restitution hearing. Since when is there cross examination at a restitution hearing? The judge said he gave him special permission. Apparently, because of the amount of damage I claimed, he felt obliged to do so. Keep in mind my homeowners insurance had already reviewed and approved the claim.

But let's go back to the courtroom. This little prosecutor guy spends at least ten minutes yelling at me about the garbage disposal having to be replaced! He wanted to know if I had tried to clean it. Let me clarify this for you. The criminal entered my home through the window over the kitchen sink. A lot of the glass landed in the garbage disposal. When we cleaned the sink we did try to turn on the disposal, but it would not work. The insurance company deemed it unsafe to try to force it since it was

Ms. Vivica

filled with glass. Maybe if I had cut my hands trying to clean it the prosecutor would have been happy.

There was also a comment about a rug I owned. The price was over a thousand dollars. The judge said I was excessive! Again, my insurance company approved the claim. It was easy considering I had the receipt, and three separate websites that listed it for the same price. How dare me for having good taste and the ability to buy expensive items for my home. The judge and prosecutor were appalled at the lavishness of my home. I was treated like I was the criminal on the stand. The district attorney never objected and never even looked up. I was verbally abused on the stand. I was yelled at, insulted, and disrespected, with no objection from the district attorney who was supposed to be there to represent me. He never asked another question.

When I stepped down, I sat next to my lawyer. I was nearly in tears and definitely in disbelief. She held my hand and spoke a few encouraging words. Anna was in the courtroom with me and she, too, supported me through this ordeal. My other supporters: Lisa, Kim and April were not it court that day. We all thought this was just to finalize the value of my loss and to determine restitution, and not an inquisition against me.

The judge ordered a measly $2,000 in restitution. The real criminal was not even there that day. The prosecutor called him by phone with the decision. He agreed to pay $200.00 per month. That was it!

After being assaulted by a crazy man, then the sheriff department, and then the court, I was exhausted but determined

3 A.M.

not to be silent. This system was one I had abided by all my life and for it not to be there when I need it was beyond disappointing. It was betrayal.

I want to stress that I do not think all law enforcement is bad. There are many people I care about working in law enforcement. They have been supportive and understanding. Most were just as confused as I was as to how this could have been handled in this matter. Some of them still reach out to check on me.

I purposely did not mention the names of the law enforcement personnel involved because it is not the main focus of my story. Their bad behavior does not warrant their names to be included in my story. They are part of a system that has been left to govern itself. None of us can be biased when the consequences may negatively impact our own lives. However, they should be held accountable for their actions. I was violated. Where was I supposed to turn if not to law enforcement?

There is pending litigation and I will once again have to rely on the court. While the sherrif's department did not commit the initial crime, they contributed to it significantly. The criminal did what criminals do, break the law. Law enforcement is supposed to uphold the law... for every citizen. I now wonder if they would even respond to a call from this address if the criminal or one of his family members returned. If so, who would they protect?

My home, the one I worked hard to purchase, decorate, and fill with family and friends, became somewhat of a prison. I was afraid to go out and afraid to stay home. If you can imagine a longtime prisoner being freed with one caveat: he must continue to live in his cell. The cell door would be unlocked and he was free to go and come as he pleased, but his home was to remain right there. How could he be expected to heal under such dire circumstances?

For many weeks after returning home from the hotel I could not turn off the lights. I stayed up most nights, feeling like I needed to be prepared to protect myself. Darkness was the enemy. It wasn't until the sun was beginning to peek through the darkness that I could trust falling asleep. I realized I had to do something. I had to stop relying on myself or law enforcement to make me feel safe. I had to go to my source, Jesus Christ. I prayed with my friend, April, throughout every room the first night I returned home. I realized I needed to do that every evening. I had to rely on Him. I do not see how anyone can make it through anything like this without HIM! I am thankful that He loves me. I am thankful He was there and will be there through it all.

Excuse me for just a second, I need a praise moment: *Thank you, Jesus! Thank you for keeping me. Thank you for protecting me. Thank you for not letting me lose my mind. Thank you for the victory. Thank you for not leaving me. Thank you for what didn't happen! My faith and my trust are in You!*

Eventually, I was able to turn off most of the lights, but they were replaced with night lights. I learned to ask for help. I was not going to get through this on my own. Most people saw me as a strong, courageous woman able to stand through anything. While that was admirable, it was not what I needed at the time. So, I had to reach out to someone who did not know me—a trained,

3 A.M.

licensed therapist. Cheryl Jones-Dix, LCSW, had no opinions or misconceptions of me. She heard me. I encourage anyone who is suffering to find a way to be heard. It is so validating. You are the victim! Yes, you lived. No, you are not black and blue. Yes, you are still taking care of day-to-day tasks, but you are hurting. If that feeling is left unchecked, you will implode.

Ms. Cheryl was not the first person I met when I was looking for a therapist, she was the third. I needed to know my story would resonate with the person I would be working with. I needed empathy not apathy. The other two therapists were great, but not a good fit for this particular need. Don't be afraid to make a few visits with different therapists or switch if for any reason you are not fully connecting with the person. You have to be in an environment where you are comfortable and can share everything. You are the patient, not the customer, and entitled to a second or third opinion if needed.

My well-meaning family and friends kept telling me I was *going to* be okay; I was *going to* be back to normal in no time; I was *going to* feel safe; I was *going to do this or that*, *going to feel this or that*; *going to*, *going to*. *Going to* was somewhere in my future, but I was stuck in my present.

This impacted every area of my life. I did not trust most people. I did not want to be around most people, but I did not want to be alone. It was a very confusing season.

It affected my work schedule tremendously. There were many days I could not get out of the bed all day. But at night, I was vigilant. My patience was very short with people. I was very abrupt in my responses. I had to be very careful when talking to clients. I tried to be polite and answer their questions and would usually try to refer them to our customer service line or a colleague. I did not want to offend anyone. I would later apologize to my team at a meeting, asking for their understanding and forgiveness if during that time I had offended them. This also created another burden, financially. I am self-employed. There is no policy to cover me from fear! I am in the insurance business. I had a policy for disability, cancer, critical illness, and anything medical. This was not any of those things. In addition, the sheriff department was an account I had spent most of my career servicing. That would no longer be an option.

Of everything that happened to me that night, the criminal has no recollection of the entire event, and law enforcement has not taken any measurable responsibility. To date, they are claiming immunity to all charges. I am the only one who was affected.

On January 23, 2014, at 3:00 A.M., I was at home, alone, and asleep. There was nothing I could have done differently. I have to believe there is a purpose. Maybe it was for me to have this new sensitivity and awareness of others who have experienced traumatic episodes and have no one to talk to, or no one to listen, or no one that really hears them. I'm listening.

What did someone/people do that helped you?

My neighbor, William Hunt, responded quickly. He helped me with the initial cleanup. I remember looking at a pool of blood on the floor and him saying, "I got it," and turning me away. He

3 A.M.

stayed until my cousin, Anna Brown, arrived. Anna staying with me beyond that was significant. My friends: Felicia Carmon, who we refer to as Lisa, Kimberly Chenier, and April Mosby were each instrumental in making me feel supported. They were with me the first day of court. Kim let me know that if this went to trial she would take off from work and be there with me. It meant the world to me to know I would not be alone. April leaving her family and spending that first night back in my home after I had left the hotel, without my asking her to do so, was priceless. Lisa stopping by regularly just to be there and making sure that I was okay was so precious. I am grateful to be surrounded by such caring and wonderful friends, sisters.

I want to point out that I did not tell my immediate family, initially. I needed them to treat me as if nothing had ever happened. I needed to feel normal somewhere. When they later learned about it, they offered their love and support. They were just as angry, confused and disappointed as me. I knew I would need to reassure them that I was all right. I had to wait until I could do that.

I'm grateful for the customer service I received by Wawanesa Insurance. They were a bright spot in an otherwise dark moment.

Petersens Carpet Care adjusted their day to clean my home so I would not have to live in the atmosphere of a crime scene.

I appreciated the prayers and words of encouragement I received after it was on the news.

Ms. Vivica

What did someone/people do that disappointed you?
The justice system.

I still cannot believe the way law enforcement and later the court system handled this case. I am hoping that we will eventually receive a favorable decision.

It was also a surprise to realize how difficult it was to find a lawyer. I contacted numerous lawyers and law firms that wanted to know if someone had been killed or severely physically injured. Since my answer was no, they could not help me. It's a shame too many wanted a presumably easy win. My attorney was outraged when she heard my story and immediately went to work on my behalf.

What could someone/people have done that would have helped you?
Without a doubt that would have to be listen. I mean *really* listen. Not just to respond or to give advice, but just listen and hear what I was saying and how I was saying it. I yearned to be heard.

The most important to me would have been to show up. I was so grateful for those who did. There were plenty of small things I would have appreciated, but would never have been able to put into words to ask for. Sometimes just having another person in the room would have been enough.

I needed people to recognize I was hurting and not my normal self. Too many were still looking for me to give something to them, perform at the optimal one hundred miles per hour speed, and address their concerns. They couldn't see that while I

3 A.M.

longed to be there for each of them, I needed them to be there for me. I needed someone to see that my temporary season had altered my current life and it was okay to grieve what I had lost in the process. I needed concern and not control.

Final Thoughts

I encourage anyone that is a friend, colleague, or family member of someone who has just experienced a traumatic experience to give them a pass on daily tasks and offer your support. I promise you will have a permanent place in their heart.

Keep praying with them and for them. It's the best way to win every battle.

Be that someone that someone needs.

About the Victor:

Ms. Vivica is the president and founder of **PRAZEUP INC.** She is an author, publisher, playwright and speaker. Her Christian Children's series, teaching the 10 Commandments featuring her character, Bmally® the Golden Lamb for God, has been taught globally. She provides teaching workshops and conferences for Children's Ministry leaders. She is a graduate of the School of Ministry at Cottonwood Church in Los Alamitos, California. She has served in ministry for over twenty-two years.

Ms. Vivica is also a licensed insurance agent/broker and owner of Valor Benefits. With over seventeen years in the insurance business, she has received many awards and has been one of the top producers year after year.

She is a volunteer and board member for many organizations.

Valor 2 Victory is her latest series. It was created to provide an outlet for others to hear stories of what could have been tragic instances in someone's life but have triumphant endings and how to help them.

"I learned that courage was not the absence of fear, but the triumph over it. The brave man is not he who does not feel afraid, but he who conquers that fear."

—Nelson Mandela

The Missing Part

In August 2001, I was shot in the head. I suppressed the exact date, but I know it was about a month before 9/11. I remember seeing the planes hitting the building on TV during my time at home.

I was in the process of rebuilding a 1963 Chevy Nova I had recently bought from Alabama. It was my restoration project. I was looking for a bell housing, which is a part of the transmission. I wanted to convert the car from an automatic to a stick shift. I had been searching around and couldn't find it. My wife has an uncle who lives in Wilmington, California who is into cars and parts and rebuilding old cars. He knew everyone in the neighborhood that worked on cars and he knew where to find parts. I told him what I needed. He was on the lookout. Sure enough, a friend of his had the part. His friend lived in Compton. We agreed to meet on a Saturday. I grabbed my son, EJ, who was three years old, and put him in the car seat in the back. I remember that it was a rental car because my car needed to be repaired. I love working on cars so I was repairing the transmission on that car, too. Actually, I stopped by my buddy's house in Long Beach for a while and visited him before heading to meet them. I think we watched some sporting event or something on TV, but mainly we were just hanging out. I left there and went to Wilmington and picked up my wife's uncle, and we drove to Compton. I bought the part. I distinctly remember thinking I didn't have any idea where I was going, but I knew I wanted to get to Compton, get the part, and get back to Wilmington to drop off my uncle before dark. My uncle knew his way around the streets so he was comfortable, I was not. We made it in good time. We left Compton and drove back to my wife's uncle's house in Wilmington just before dusk.

I pulled over to let him out. He lived in a duplex, but we had to stop two houses before his because we couldn't park anywhere else. We chatted for a while. With his legs out of the door, he hopped out of the car, and just as he turned, I said, "I'll see you later." As I am looking at him, we heard a sound (thump) like a rock hitting a window. We were quiet for a minute. He looked over his shoulder at me. We were both thinking, *What the heck was that?* I pointed to the windshield and we noticed and discussed that it looked like a bullet hole.

My uncle said, "You're right. Look at this." He could see little residual pieces of glass in the car.

I said, "It is a bullet hole. That was right in front of my face." I reached up and touched my face and looked at my hand. I didn't feel anything but a little pressure in my head. Then I really looked around. There was blood all over the place. My first response was to check my son because he was right behind me. Had I'd been six inches to either side it would have hit him. I got out the car. My uncle went to call 911. The fire department and paramedics arrived and put me in the ambulance. I knew I had been shot in the head.

The Missing Part

When they put me in the ambulance, it was kind of weird. A peace came over me and, I thought, *This is it*. I asked the paramedic, "Am I going to die?"

He tried to give me a pep talk.

I said, "Look man, it's cool, I need to know. Am I going to die?"

The paramedic shrugged and said he didn't know.

At that point I made my peace with the Lord. I prayed. I don't remember my prayers exactly, but basically it was to please take me home and make sure to look after my family. That's where I was. I was praying for my safety, but mostly for my family. I was okay with it. I don't remember the pain or anything.

The next thing I remember was being in the emergency room. They took me to Harbor UCLA Medical Center. I saw nurses and doctors. They cut off all my clothes, rolled me over and checked for bullet holes. Then they gave me morphine. They just covered me and left me there. I didn't see anyone for a long while. I was left in the triage area with the curtain drawn.

The next people I saw were from Los Angeles Police Department (LAPD). Two officers showed up. They were asking me questions. They asked what I was doing in Wilmington, who I knew there, and why I was there. It was really insensitive. They treated me like a gang member that got what he deserved. So you got shot, so what. I was offended. I told them that I didn't know anyone other than my wife's uncle. They kept asking. I told them what we had done that day.

One of the cops said, "You know they call that part of town ghost town, right?" I didn't catch what that meant. Then they told me it referred to the area being known for gangs, shootings, murders and dead people… ghost town. That was it. They left.

I think the drugs I was given kicked in and things were becoming foggy. I had to go take some test. I remember taking an MRI.

My wife and brother–in-law showed up.

My eyesight in my right eye was blurry. I had double and triple vision. I had more tests overnight.

The next morning they gave me a prescription of prednisone and codeine-3 and sent me home. They told me to come back for a check-up in seventeen days.

I slept sitting up in my recliner.

Even now it impacts the right side of my face. I have nerve damage. When I get tired it may sound like I'm drunk, I'm not. I have to make sure my lips are moving correctly so I can pronounce all my words.

After being home for a few days, I was not getting any better. My wife kept saying we need to go back to the hospital and I kept saying no. I was in so much pain, and then my face started to turn black. After day five, I conceded and went to the hospital—Long Beach Memorial. They responded immediately.

By that time, my right eye had dropped so low that it was level with the bridge of my nose.

My family physician arrived and brought an eye specialist who specializes in orbital surgery. I still have to see him every two years.

The reason I hadn't been able to sleep was the bullet was lodged in my brain. My brain was leaking and swelling. The

The Missing Part

pressure wouldn't allow me to lie down. They put an IV in and pumped me up with prednisone and morphine. I had a bad infection. My eye was closed and filled with puss. The nurse had to clean it every hour. I stayed in the hospital for about five days to get the swelling and the infection under control before they could even perform the surgery I needed. I had to have outpatient surgery and reconstructive surgery.

The sad part is if I had waited the seventeen days for my appointment at LAC-UCLA Medical Center, if I had lived that long, it would have been too late for that type of surgery.

The surgeon told me it had to be within ten days of the accident before bones start mending on their own. Basically, I would have been permanently disfigured or they would have had to break my face and try to fix it. The only thing holding my eye in place was the fat and muscle because my bone structure was no longer in place. So I made it just in time. The surgery went well.

While I was in the hospital, different specialists would come in—neurosurgeons, plastic surgeons and others. I will never forget the one time they put an x-ray up for me to see. The bone in my head literally stopped the bullet from fully penetrating my brain. They would call people in to look and say they didn't know how I made it. One of them said, "It's a good thing you have them good thick African bones."

I kept asking, "Am I going to live?" They still didn't know. They said if I made it past the next six months I would probably be okay.

The bullet is still lodged behind my right eye. It was jammed in my brain, but the bone stopped it from going all the way through. The bullet also acted as a plug and it stopped the leak in my brain. That's why they said six months. In six months my body would have it encapsulated.

It caused some nerve damage, but it didn't affect my motor skills. It only impacted my speech. Outside of that, I've been good. Things worked out.

It isn't a place you would want to be in, but it was a blessing that I was able to be at home and relax.

First of all, I had Colonial Life Disability Insurance from working at LA County USC Medical Center. I remember when I worked in the women's hospital side they always had signs about victims of violent crimes. I had just had a conversation about victims of violent crime about a week before this happened. Somebody explained it to me. I called the hospital staff. They had a special fund that helped with my medical bills and my salary. That really helped. That was a blessing. I wondered if I was going to live or die, but I was not worried or stressed about my bills.

About a month later, I received a call from LAPD asking more questions. It lasted about five minutes and that was it. They did explain what happened that day. We got caught in a drive-by shooting. The car with the shooter was travelling on the north/southbound street and we were on an east/westbound street. They were shooting into the street as they passed the intersection. We were in the crossfire. The target was two houses from where we were. They were shooting toward the house. They told me the car I was driving had five or six bullet holes. I didn't know that because I had not seen it. It was a rental car. They also found fifteen or sixteen shells on the street. I didn't remember hearing any of that. I just remember that one bullet.

They said it was a Hispanic gang, Mexican gang. I didn't see anything and I had no idea.

Another thing, I have never, even to this day, felt vengeful. I never thought about getting a gun and trying to shoot at anybody. We can say "God said this" and "God said that," but you never really know how you are going to react when something happens.

This was one of those situations. What am I going to do? Would this make me be a reckless person? Or, would I just trust God to take care of it? I trusted God.

I have never been mad, then or now. I have never felt sorry for myself. I never had a pity party. Never asked, "Why me God?" I never felt like that. I had to go forward.

It was my last year of college. It was just before school started. I couldn't half see and I couldn't sit up for very long. I thought, *If I'm going to die, at least let me finish college.* I wanted to give my kids some inspiration that if you have faith and keep moving you can get it done.

I knew that if I missed roll call they would drop me so I sent my brother-in-law to sit in for me the first day to answer to my name. He couldn't believe I wanted to go to school with everything that was happening. I didn't know if I was going to live, but I had never missed school and I wasn't going to start now.

The next week I was determined to go, but I still couldn't drive or see clearly. So, my wife would take me to class and take notes. I would sit there with my eyes closed. If my eyes were open too long my head would hurt. It's a good thing that I am an auditory learner. I could learn by listening. I jotted down a few notes here and there. My wife stayed with me the first three or four weeks then she returned to work.

I rode the bus for the rest of the semester. I didn't even try to drive, for the safety of myself and others. The doctors had told me that there was a possibility I would have seizures. Even though I still had my license I didn't want to take that chance. I didn't want to be behind the wheel. I got used to the bus. It didn't really bother me.

I would sit in the back of the class with my eyes closed and listen. Every now and then I would open my eyes long enough to take a few notes then shut them again. I never said anything to the teacher. I wanted to be treated like everyone else. I didn't miss a beat.

I got my bachelor's degree in May of that year.

We all say we believe, but who are you really? I believe if God takes care of the birds and the bees, He'll take care of me. He can take care of you of your needs, but if you want the things you desire, are you willing to put in the work for it?

I never wanted my kids to have any excuses. When they have a little bump and don't want to go to school, I just look at them and say, "I had a bullet in my head. So, what's your problem again?" That ends that conversation.

Faith without works is dead sounds simple, but it's big.

I did have some reservations about revisiting that neighborhood. For about three years after that I did not go near that area. I re-routed myself to prevent it. Sometimes I had to take the bridge to go around or freeway connections that did not pass through that area. It was an eerie feeling. It was more of anxiety, I suppose.

I feel that even though I had gone there for a specific reason I always felt like I wasn't supposed to be there. So after that happened I began feeling anxiety and I paid attention to those feelings.

It wasn't until the father of my co-worker passed away and his service was going to be at a church in Wilmington that I would have to make a decision to go into that city. I was not comfortable. I rationalized that it was going to be in broad daylight, I was going with a group of people from work, and it was church.

As I headed in that direction, there was some discomfort. I kept those feelings to myself. Once we arrived, there was still anxiety, but I was able to settle down for the service and not think about it. Once I went outside after the service it resurfaced, but not as strong as it had been when we arrived. The longer we stayed outside the more bearable it became. I was able to hold conversations and not feel that tension.

After a while the uncomfortable feelings subsided. The ride back to work was fine. I believe that was the day I was able to overcome the anxiety. But, I still tend to stay on the main highway and not stop at gas stations or convenience stores near that area. I continue to trust God. My motto is: Pray and get up every day. He'll take care of you.

Eric Ross

What did someone/people do that really helped you?

I worked at LA County USC Medical Center. I didn't realize how much my coworkers and bosses admired me. When you are out for an extended time you can lose your benefits and your seniority. They donated so much of their sick time, totaling about two months that I didn't lose anything.

What did someone/people do that really disappointed you?

We had some unfinished projects going on at my house. We had just added a family room and some other things. This was still within the first month that I had gone home and I was still fuzzy. I had stopped taking my pain medicine because it left me so cloudy. I didn't want to leave any unfinished business. I wanted everything done. I think some people may have taken advantage of me.

What could someone/people have done that would have helped you?

The hospital treated me like a gang member. I was not. I was not dressed like a gang member. I didn't have anything that would have given them that impression. They just made that assumption. I didn't deserve that. I had two very good insurances, one from LA County and the other from my wife's employer. I think I was stereotyped because of my skin color and the fact that my wound was from a gunshot. I felt like they just left me alone to die. They cut my clothes, rolled me over, then covered me up and disappeared. Then the cops talked to me like I was thug. They gave me a few drugs and sent me home and said come back in three weeks. I had a nine millimeter bullet in my head. Had I followed their instructions I would have died.

Final Thoughts

When it's all said and done, I'm okay. I have 20/20 vision. The only reason I wear glasses is because the injury created a stigmatism.

There was a peace I had when I thought I was passing, I really felt like I would go home to see the Lord. Whenever your day comes, and it can come swiftly like a thief in the night, you need to be ready. You can't wait until something happens and then say, "Hey, Lord!" You might not have that opportunity.

I knew that was where that peace came from. It wasn't my first conversation with the Lord. I would just say to anyone, find your peace with the Lord now.

About the Victor:

Eric L. Ross Sr., MBA is a Financial Consultant who founded Ross Wealth Management Group, a private consulting and planning firm, to provide unbiased financial and investment advice to his clients. He has been in practice and servicing his clientele for over a decade.

Eric holds the following licenses: FINRA Securities Series 24, 7, 63, 66 and California Insurance.

Eric Ross

He is a native of Indiana and currently resides in Long Beach, California with his wife of over twenty years, Onica. He has three daughters, one son, and two granddaughters.

Eric can be contacted at eric@erossgroup.com or 562-206-0675.

"Never worry about numbers. Help one person at a time, and always start with the person nearest you."

—Mother Teresa

Off Campus

It was a Thursday afternoon. Spring was coming. It had been warm that day. I hummed to myself as I walked home. My meeting had just ended. My first semester of senior year had been put to bed, and I was well into my second; graduation was on the horizon. The sun looked particularly beautiful that day. It danced over the soccer field on one side and apartment buildings on the other. The church bells chimed in the distance. I stood at the corner of Turk and Parker waiting to cross the street. A light breeze brushed my rosy cheek as the music from one of my earphones harmonized with the golden rays of the sun. I was reflecting on my college journey.

Twenty more seconds until I can cross the street.

I moved away from home and settled in a place I had always dreamed of living. I made my mark at school. I accomplished major goals and mastered the art of time management. Yes, that day was a good day.

Twelve seconds until I can cross the street.

I continued to think back to all the friends I had made. Life was grand and I thought to myself: *It's good to be me.* I considered myself to be so blessed. I was in awe of how wonderful my life had turned out. The light at the intersection was yellow. The signal changed and I could now walk across the street. I looked to my left and saw the majestic Lone Mountain; shrubbery and bushes knelt at its feet. On the mountain top was an old Victorian Chapel that once housed Jesuit priests that are now classrooms. Observing that view, I pinched myself and thought: *You lucky girl.* I turned the corner to walk down the one-hundred-twenty-foot hill on my way home.

Seventy feet away, I saw a man walking uphill toward me. I was unsuspecting and unexplainably at peace. Cars zoomed by and children squealed. They were dressed for a swim meet that was happening in the gym across the street. Trees sleepily extended their branches as if wanting to greet me and shake my hand.

Now the man and I were fifty feet apart. I could see the details of his clothing. *Raiders fan.* I remembered my first Raiders game and how my dad drove from Los Angeles to San Diego with my little brother and me. I missed my daddy. My backpack interrupted my memories. It was heavy because of my laptop. I wish I could have taken it out of my backpack, but then I would have had to carry it. *I will be home soon,* I thought. *It's not that bad.*

Twenty feet closer and the man caught my eye. His bright blue, cold, beady eyes made me uneasy. I walked a little slower to keep the distance between us. I didn't want to assume anything because of his attire. *Just ignore him and he will walk past me,* I coached myself.

Ten feet. I looked up. He was staring directly into my eyes. I looked to my left and there were parked cars. The narrow sidewalk would not allow me to pass him on that side. I looked to my right. There was a sandy area that I wasn't sure I could run through without losing my footing. *What is this guy doing?* I was trying to figure a way to move from his path, but there weren't any good options. I cautiously continued on.

Five feet. I moved to my right. He moved to his left. I moved to my left, he moved to his right. I thought we were having that awkward moment when two people are trying to figure how to let the other pass, while they look like they are doing a stiff and fractured waltz. However, instead of asking me to dance, he was trying to barricade me. *Okay, something is about to happen.* An internal danger alert consumed me. He continued stalking his prey—me. His stare was becoming more intense. I could not move. I was paralyzed by fear. Where was he trying to go?

I wanted to believe he was just going to pass me by, but I knew better.

Five inches away, face to face. I tried to move around him, but he gently grabbed my shoulder. I was surprised that his touch was more intrusive than forceful. His stare was intense.

His hat matched his jersey and his black jeans were sagging low. He wore a gold cross chain. The jersey was so big on his wiry frame, but I could tell he had strength. I looked into his eyes. They were dilated. *He is out of it, and he is either drunk or on drugs. My guess would be drugs.*

Only seconds passed, but they felt like the longest seconds of my life. My heart was racing. I had to do something. I put my hand on his chest and told him, "No… No… Stop."

Anonymous

He paused for a moment and lifted his hand. *Okay, I have a chance to get out of this. He is moving so slow. If he were going to harm me he would have done so.* He put his hand back on my shoulder, and my hand remained on his chest to keep him at a distance. His hand slowly reached for his jersey.

This is it. He is going to pull a gun out of his pants, and he is going to rob me. I have my laptop, phone, and iPod. My thoughts shifted. *He is going to kill me. He will shoot me... I am going to die... Okay God, I am ready. I am sorry I didn't get to do all of the things You needed me to do.*

He slowly pulled up his shirt and pulled out his penis. I was somewhat relieved it was not a gun, but still in shock; being a virgin, this was the first time I had seen a man's penis directed at me. I moved his hand from my shoulder and pushed him. The push was strong enough to make him stumble because of his sagging pants and the steep incline. Gravity was working against him, and me. I turned to run back to campus. I wanted to turn around to see how closely he was following me, but I could not. I was afraid that looking back would slow me down. The weight of the laptop in my backpack was already doing that. *I am not going to make it. I need something faster than me. Cars!*

I saw a car pull up to the stop sign. I quickly moved to get the driver's attention. There was an Asian couple in the car. I banged on their window.

"Stop the car! Stop the car! Stop! Let me in," I screamed.

The car zoomed off, and left me stranded. I was terrified. I kept running. Then, I saw a woman getting into a red car. I ran to the woman, and said, "Help me! Help me! He is going to attack me!" The woman looked up, as she was getting into the car, and told me to get in. I jumped into the back seat, and looked at the man's face. As the woman drove away, his stare became enraged. I was trying to regain my composure.

"Call the police!" the woman yelled.

My fingers trembled as I dialed 911.

"911, what's your emergency?" the female dispatcher asked.

"Hello my name is ******. I am on Parker and Turk. There is a white male walking up Turk looking to flash young women. Please send someone. There are children around."

I thought if he was assaulting women, then the children waiting for their swim meet could also be in danger.

"What is your current location?" The dispatcher asked. I told her I was in the car with someone and on my way home. I gave her my address. She said officers would meet me there.

I looked to my right and saw a small, blonde-haired boy with apple cheeks and wide eyes. He held a book in his hands. He was confused as to what was going on.

He can't be more than four or five years old. He is precious. I am sorry to have to interrupt his innocence like this.

The woman pulled over, turned around and asked, "Are you okay?"

I looked up and said, "Yes, I am all right. Thank you so much for stopping."

"I am glad you came to me. I saw him with his penis out as he was walking up the hill and I wanted to get my little boy in the car as soon as possible."

I thanked the woman one more time and gathered my things to get out of the car. I felt bad for imposing on that family. I did not want to make my problems their problems.

The woman stopped me and asked, "Do you want me to take you home? I see you are a student. You can't live too far from here." I accepted her offer.

I sat in awe and was overwhelmed by the kindness of this Good Samaritan. I buckled the seat belt and thanked the woman once more. I gave her directions to where I lived.

Thirty minutes since I had crossed the street. In thirty minutes my life had gone from a quiet, drama-free, fun-filled life, to a whirlwind of chaos, and sexual assault. I went from feeling proud of myself and all the goals I had accomplished to being ready and making peace with the fact that I could have died a traumatic death. It was all so much to process.

I got out of the woman's car and ran into my apartment. My roommate and landlord had been sitting at our table with company. I saw two bewildered faces looking back at me. My landlord ran to my aid as I slumped toward the floor in tears. She guided me to the living room as she excused herself from her company. I told her everything and explained that the police would be on their way to get my statement.

After I took a few deep breaths, I reassured her I was okay and I was going to call my parents to let them know what happened.

I went into my bedroom and closed the door behind me to call my father. His cell phone began to ring.

"Hello?" my father answered.

"Hi, Daddy," I spoke as I tried to stop more tears.

"Hey, what's going on?"

My father could have never guessed what his youngest daughter was about to tell him.

"Daddy, I have to tell you something, and I need you to step outside for a minute because it is serious." I knew this time of day my dad, a barber, would be in his shop.

I could hear the clippers in the background cut off and I knew he was moving toward the door.

"I was grabbed by a flasher today. I am okay; he only touched my arm and waved his penis at me, but the cops will be here to get my statement in a few minutes."

Knowing my father, I had to present all the facts at once to minimize his panic. There was a pause and I heard him take a breath.

"You were grabbed by a flasher?"

"Yes, I—"

My landlord knocked on the bedroom door. The cops had arrived.

"Let me call you back, Daddy, the cops are here. I just wanted to let you know I am okay."

As a tear rolled down my face, I was hoping he could not hear the fear in my voice.

"Okay, call me back when you can."

Forty-five minutes since I had crossed the street.

Two cops were standing at the door.

"Hi, ma'am. This is detective ****, and I am officer ****. I understand that you made a call today reporting an incident off Turk. Do you mind if we come in to talk to you?"

"No, please, come in."

I sat on the couch as I told the officers what I had experienced. To talk about it aloud sounded foreign to me. I just wanted peace again. They continued to talk to me, but I heard nothing until one of them said, "Would you mind coming with us in our squad car to identify the perp?"

"Yes to all of your questions," I politely replied.

Now that was something I was not expecting to happen. I gathered my things to walk down the stairs to the car.

Am I really about to get in the back of a cop car to go back to this man that just tried to grab me? I have to. This should not happen to anyone else. I'd rather identify him and prevent this from happening to another individual.

The squad car returned to the scene. The man had been arrested and even in handcuffs. He tried to break free twice. *Clearly he is out of his mind*, I thought. There was a crowd of cops surrounding him.

I looked out the window to see a young lady with whom I had dance class. We recognized one another. The cops kept us separated. I was not allowed to get out of the car.

I was bombarded with question after question.

"Is this the hat he wore? What about the chain? Is this the chain you described?" the cops inquired.

The officer driving the car was ordered to drive closer.

I told him, "I don't want to go any further. I don't want him to see my face again."

Off Campus

He stopped the car. My wishes were conflicting with what the commander on the scene was ordering him to do.

The man was sitting handcuffed on a sidewalk about thirty feet away.

"I don't want to go any further, please," I said a little more firmly.

The officer driving turned around and asked, "Can you tell me if this is the man you described?"

"Yes, I can."

"How?"

"Because I have twenty-twenty vision and I can see every detail from here. His jersey is the same, the hat is the same, and I have already identified the chain they brought over. When he grabbed me, I was taking in all of these details. He has blue eyes, blonde hair cut low, and high cheek bones. He has a sharp nose and beady eyes and small teeth. When a stranger pulls their penis out for you to see, intending to harm you, you don't forget their face."

I was irritated at the question. The cop turned around and raised his eyebrows. He seemed to be impressed with my response. He continued to roll forward until he was about ten feet from the flasher. I knew he was trying to do his job, but I was annoyed he didn't listen to my saying I felt unsafe.

I pulled my hood over my head to cover my face.

They asked me to write the statement. I complied. When I completed the statement, one of the detectives responded that he couldn't understand what I had written. He needed to talk to me.

He sounded irritated. I felt like he was a bonehead and lacked sensitivity, but I took a deep breath and complied.

I felt vulnerable being a Black, young lady in the midst of a bunch of White cops and so I did my best to do everything they asked. The thought might not have been politically correct, but in reality no one is politically correct when it comes to racial tension and misogyny.

One hour and fifteen minutes since the signal changed, and I had crossed the street.

Dusk had fallen. Still in the squad car, the female police officer drove me back home after I identified the street corner where the incident had taken place. I was disappointed at how careless the police had handled a fragile situation, but since when did the law enforcement care about people's feelings?

I walked through the door of my apartment. I was drained. I looked at my cell phone and had two missed calls from my parents. I knew I needed to call them or they would remain worried. I called my mom as I plopped down on my bed. I told her everything. I was tired of talking about it. I just wanted to take a shower and go to bed. After a long conversation and reassuring my mom I was okay, I hung up and dragged myself to take a bath.

My landlord was concerned and drew a bath for me. It was what I needed at that moment.

Four hours since I had crossed the street.

While sitting in the tub with bubbles surrounding me and my knees tucked up to my chin, there was a knock at the door. My landlord went to answer it. I heard mumbling and then a knock at the bathroom door. My landlord let me know the cop, who ignored my request in the car, was at the door asking for a signature. I reached for my towel, got out of the tub and went to the front door. I poked my head through the cracked door to speak with the officer who was standing on the walkway. He handed me the paper to sign through the cracked door. His presence threw me back into a mental battle of trying to keep calm and trying not to cry. I just wanted to be left alone for a few moments of peace.

After signing the paper, I got back in the tub and cried. That was the one moment in the whole day where I could just let it all out and not have to worry about imposing on anyone. That was a moment I needed.

After my bath, I crawled into bed, heavy with anticipation of the pillow supporting my head. I fell asleep immediately.

However, my peace was short lived. Throughout the night, I tossed and turned. I kept seeing his face. The man, the flasher had infiltrated my subconscious. I had dreams that he was standing over my bed ready to grab me. I would snap out of my slumber to find that I was alone in my room. This happened five times throughout the night.

I woke up the next morning with tears rolling down my face. I could not keep myself from crying. I was hysterical. I was scared to leave my room and scared to leave the apartment. The four walls in my room had been closing in on me. I felt like I was having a nervous breakdown. This was going to be a long road to recovery. I decided to make an appointment with the school counselor that morning.

I called a friend and asked if he could walk me. He was on his way to a counseling meeting so he was regrettably not available. I assured him I would be fine.

I realized we were all students and busy. I was going to have to do this on my own. I was scared out of my mind, but I got dressed, put on my shoes, and walked out the door.

I waited for the Munibus to arrive. We headed toward my school and I noticed that almost everyone was wearing a hat. That freaked me out! Everywhere I looked I saw that guy wearing that stupid hat.

That was an unfamiliar feeling for me. Terrified, paralyzed, just at the sight of a hat.

I tried to keep calm until I could get to the school counselor's office.

The session was productive. I made major breakthroughs in a matter of an hour and I was feeling better. I had ridden in the back of a cop car, identified the perpetrator, made an appointment to meet with a counselor, walked to school all alone, and I had done it on my own. Yet, I had never been alone. Christ was with me the entire time.

Meanwhile, I had been getting phone calls from my father. He is not great at handling moments of high stress and was not dealing with this situation well at all.

While I was speaking with the counselor, he had a customer in his barber's chair that was sharing her experience of being raped. He was wondering if there were any parallels between her story and my story. He needed to hear my voice. He needed to know that his baby girl was okay and he needed details. Details I was not ready to give. I couldn't relive that moment again. I had counted on my mother to fill him in, but she had not. I had to make the difficult decision to end the conversation without answering his questions. That broke my heart because I wanted him to know. I wanted him to protect me, but I knew the distance between us would not allow it. So, I simply said, "I love you, Daddy," and hung up.

My father and I are really close. He is the type of man that loves being the protector and provider for his family. He, too, hated feeling vulnerable, something we have in common, and when he realized that there was nothing he could do he began to panic.

Sexual assault is any type of forced or coerced sexual contact or behavior that happens without consent. Sexual assault includes rape and attempted rape, child molestation, and sexual harassment or threats.

It is important to note here that, in my opinion, when someone has been sexually assaulted, they are not the only one experiencing stress. Your closest loved ones are also experiencing stress. They, too, need a platform where they can talk and ask questions. It is equally important to know the appropriate time and ways to address those needs.

The first days, and sometimes months, after the attack is crucial. For me, it was three days. Therefore, I suggest you pay attention to their behavior after the attack. I use the pronoun "their" because I do not want to say victims. We are survivors.

It is a time to extend grace and understanding. Family and friends need time to process that a loved one was attacked and that they were not there to protect them. It is a difficult situation for everyone.

I urge everyone to talk to someone, be it a family member or a professional, just talk.

To conclude this story, I want to say that I am fine. I have graduated from college with a Bachelor of Arts degree in Communication. I have moved back to my hometown and I am in the process of making a niché for myself. I am starting my career, and everything has turned out for the best.

What did someone/people do that really helped you?

I told one of my closest friends what happened that day. She worked across town at a demanding job, went to school full time, and still made time to show up. When she heard the distress in my voice, she told me she was going to come over. She was going to pick up dinner and afterward I would have her undivided attention. She listened. She was the only one that did not run away. I am eternally grateful for her kindness. She helped me move past my shock by allowing me to talk without interruptions. She understood what I needed most was empathy. She made sure I was okay and continued to check in on me after that evening.

I was surprised at how fast I bounced back, and how much of an impact it had on my life. To this day, it is hard for me to walk alone, and it is hard for me to be in my house alone at night. I am uneasy in parking structures/lots, and I find myself looking over my shoulder when I am out. I am also surprised at how my fight or flight instincts kicked in, and I am surprised at how quickly I came to terms to losing my life when I thought he was going to pull a gun. It is amazing at how quickly your mind will work when you are in a fight or flight situation. However, I am more confident. I know my capabilities. Although there is still work for me to do, I have done the hardest part.

What did someone/people do that really disappointed you?

I was most disappointed with how people responded/reacted to the news of my experience.

I explained to my professors what happened and why I missed class the next day, and one of them laughed in my face. They did later apologize to the inappropriateness of their reaction. I found that people tend to not know how to react without projecting themselves in the situation. I told friends (or people I considered to be friends) and their response was they didn't know what to say. Sometimes it is okay to say nothing. In a moment of disclosure, for me, it is best to sit and listen in silence. When in doubt, ask what the person needs. It may simply be to have someone to sit with them.

My roommate/landlord helped in the moment, but then a week later made a really inappropriate comment and told me to get over it.

One thing you should not do in a delicate situation is tell people how to feel, or what they should do, or how you would have reacted.

You should not tell people how to feel because: Who are you to tell anyone how to feel?

Everyone handles emotional stress differently. No one knows how he or she would respond until they have experienced it. Phrases like, "I would have done…," "I would have said…," and "If I were in your shoes…" are not appropriate.

What could someone/people have done that would have helped you?

I wish more people would have reacted like my friend. I was terrified and people treated me as though I was to blame and being dramatic. They would not have to say they were sorry about what happened because the offender of my peace had been placed in handcuffs. I needed someone to sit with me and say it was okay to be scared, to remind me I was justified in feeling the way I felt. I wish more people understood that actions speak louder than words.

I am not a person that shows vulnerability easily. If I reach out, it should tell you how much I value your presence in my life. It is not to be taken lightly. I needed sincerity and consistency.

If you experienced trauma, listen to me and believe me, it will get better. You are strong enough to get help. I understand what you are feeling. Most of all, do not believe you are alone. Find a close circle of friends you can be vulnerable with. I found that returning to my routine helped me find and redefine my normal.

Final Thoughts

Overall, this experience has made me stronger. I am proud I did not crumble. I took action. I did something to bring justice to my situation. I was empowered to do so by making the situation bigger than myself and speaking up. I did not want this to happen to anyone else.

If you know someone that has experienced trauma please keep my story in mind.

I want to urge people to fight to live. Fight to be resilient. Fight for your smile. Fight to get up when you feel down. Fight for your voice. Speak up, be seen, and fight to be heard even when people fight against you to keep you silent.

About the Victor:

The victor has chosen to be anonymous. This event happened in the spring of 2015. She is concerned with the offender having access to her information, but wanted to share her story. I applaud her courage.

She graduated with honors from the University of San Francisco with a Communication major and Dance minor. She is living with her family and working with a prominent insurance firm.

"We have to confront ourselves. Do we like what we see in the mirror? And, according to our light, according to our understanding, according to our courage, we will have to say yea or nay—and rise!"

—Dr. Maya Angelou

Unwanted Passenger

I had just gotten off work at a popular pizza parlor in downtown Chicago. It was a late night. I was nineteen years old. My mother was expecting me to go straight home, but I had other plans. I wanted to go see Danny.

I pulled into his neighborhood, but because it was dark, I could not see the addresses. I saw a guy walking down the street. I assumed he was one of Danny's neighbors. Very gullibly, I rolled the window down and asked, "Excuse me, do you know what that address is?" pointing to the curb.

He stopped and asked, "Who you looking for, baby?"

"Danny."

"Yeah, yeah, yeah, that's my boy, he lives right over there." He pointed across the street.

"Thank you."

I parked near where he was pointing. As I pulled in, I noticed he was walking toward my car. Even though I was rolling up the windows on my old school, two-door Lincoln my grandmother had just bought me, I didn't lock the doors. He came up to the passenger side. Naïvely I thought, *He must need a ride.*

He opened the door and quickly got inside. He looked at me and said, "Drive." His eyes were really glassy, like he was in some trance state. He looked a little on the crazy side or either very high on drugs.

Thinking quickly, I told him, "Danny owes me some money. I'm just going to go get that money and I'll be right back."

I put my hand on the door to open it and he said, "Drive, bitch, or I'll kill you." He reached into his pocket as if he were pulling out a knife or something. I was too afraid to see it, so I looked away and drove off.

The minute I drove off, I heard a voice, which I believe was either the Holy Spirit or an Angel, say to me calmly, "You have to let someone know what is going on. Make a scene."

As I drove away, he touched me. He put his hand down my shirt and fondled my breasts. I was wearing a short skirt and he put his hand under my skirt and touched my panties. He started noticing my jewelry and began removing each piece. It all happened so fast. It was just a block away from where it all started.

I looked down the street for another car or anything to come. On my left there was a row of houses, but there wasn't anyone around. It was like I was in a deserted area. Then all of a sudden, a pair of headlights came toward me. I had this sense of urgency to let that particular person know that I needed help. Instantly, I braced myself and drove into the front of their car. The other driver crashed into me with a look of shock on his face. The guy in the car with me was livid, cussing at me and calling me names. I didn't care. My focus was to get the attention of the driver in the other car. He hit the passenger side of my car where this crazy man was sitting. The driver of the other car was stunned.

Unfortunately, I would find out later that he was driving a new car that he had just bought.

I started to physically fight with the crazy guy that was in the car with me. He was mad at me for causing an accident. I jumped onto the door from inside the car and sat on the window. My arms were flailing outside the car and I was screaming to the top of my lungs, "Help me, help me, oh my God, he's trying to kill me." I was trying to get the driver of the other car to get out of his car and help me.

The crazy guy tried to push me out of the window. I got angry and I punched him in his head! We started tussling with each other as he jumped in my seat and proceeded to try drive off with me sitting in the window because he couldn't push me out. He tried desperately to drive off, but the car would not move. I was screaming. He was screaming. I felt like I was in a movie scene.

The driver of the other car jumped out, pulled out a gun, pointed it at the crazy guy, and yelled, "Freeze, police!" He was a Cook County Sheriff who had just gotten off duty.

The crazy guy couldn't get out on my side because I was still sitting in the window. He went back to the passenger side, jumped out of the window, climbed over the hood of the other man's car and dropped all my jewelry on the ground.

I yelled to the Sherriff, "Shoot him! Shoot him!"

He responded, "I can't!"

I remember thinking, *Why not?* I knew why. I knew better. My mother was a police officer and protocol was you couldn't shoot someone in the back. Well, that was the rule back in the day. It's hard to tell what the rules are now. However, at that moment, I wanted him to shoot this man in the leg or something to stop him so he wouldn't do the same thing or something worse to someone else.

The crazy guy got away. He wasn't even running. He was jogging across the street. I watched him disappear in the darkness and get away.

The driver of the other car confessed that he thought it was a staged high-jacking, which is why he delayed in helping me. He apologized and said, "I thought you guys were trying to scam me. I thought you were trying to carjack me."

People started coming out of their homes. A lady asked, "Baby, you okay? I heard you screaming all the way down the street. I live two blocks away and I heard you screaming."

I thought to myself, *You heard me and you are just now coming out?!* Thank you.

Someone else said, "I wasn't coming out there with that crazy man."

I had this conversation over and over with different people. The block was now filled with people. Some of them confessed that they were in their windows watching. Not one person called the police.

We called or had someone to call the police.

Finally, Danny came out. He heard me, too. He said he didn't know it was me.

I said, "You knew I was coming to visit. You should've been looking out for me."

Unwanted Passenger

I called my mother and told her what happened. She said, "Sure, Trisha, sure. You're coming home this late because you've been out doing something."

"No, really, Mom."

She did not believe me until I made it home with the police report. When I walked through the door and handed it to her she broke down in tears of relief. She knew what had been happening to a lot of young ladies at that time and realized it could have happened to me. Dan Ryan Woods was a place where women's dead bodies were being found weekly. Many of them had been raped. I was near that area.

I knew in my spirit that drugged up or crazy man was going to rape me and possibly kill me. I knew he had evil intentions the minute I looked into his eyes.

The next day, because my car was still there, my mother drove me out that way to see the car and look for the criminal. She wanted to see how much damage had been done to my car and she really wanted to try to find the man that had jumped in my car. I did not think that would happen. I thought, *There is no way in the world we are going to find this guy.*

She saw another fellow officer who I thought was arresting a guy. She knew the officer and I just happen to know the guy I assumed was being arrested. She told the officer what happened the night before. He said he would look around as soon as he was finished.

As we were driving and passing by men, my mother kept asking, "Is that him?"

And I would say, "No, Mom, that's not him."

About a block later, I saw a guy that fit the exact description of the guy from the night before who jumped in my car.

This guy was carrying a small brown paper bag. I remembered at that moment that the crazy man had a small brown bag, too.

So I said, "I think that's him."

"Trisha, are you sure?"

"Yes, I think that's him."

In fact, the guy actually looked at us, and he looked nervous. He saw me looking at him. He looked directly into my eyes. He didn't have that same glassy look like the night before though.

My mother made a U-turn in the middle of the street and went back to the on-duty police officer. He followed us back to find this guy. We caught up with him walking. He had made it another block or so. We turned left in front of him, just like most police do when they catch someone they have been looking for. They pinned him in and my mother and the officer jumped out of the car.

The officer pulled his weapon and they were yelling, "Get down! Get down right now!"

The guy was asking, "What did I do? What'd I do?"

He was shaking and he had his hands up. He got on the ground. He looked up at me and started crying, "Ma'am, please, whatever it was I didn't do it. I have a family. I didn't do it."

The man was crying so hard I started crying, too. Now I was confused. I was unsure.

My mother told me, "You better get it together and get it together fast. This is what they do. They act like they didn't do it and they cry crocodile tears to make you feel sorry for them. Don't you believe that bull crap."

The next thing I knew, there was a woman walking down the street. She came out of nowhere straight toward me. I think she was holding a *Watch Tower* magazine. I thought that was odd because she was alone. Normally, when you see a Jehovah's Witness they are in pairs or groups. In a very calm voice she said, "Daughter, what's wrong?"

Through my tears I gave her a brief synopsis of what had happened the night before and what was happening right then with this man on the ground. She seemed completely unfazed by the drama unfolding right there in front of us. I just felt like it was okay to talk to her. I was friendly anyway, but it was something about her that made me feel comfortable. I was so young and gullible. I knew my mother was zoned in on catching this guy, so it was nice to have a compassionate ear to hear what I was saying.

My mother and the other officer were taking care of business. They scared me.

I told the lady, "I'm not sure that's the guy that got in my car last night."

The lady said, "Trust me, when the time is right, God will reveal it to you." Then she gave me a sweet smile and walked away.

We went to the police station. I remember the detective telling me that this man had a rap sheet and that he had done some things. "All you have to do is say the word," he said.

I said, "I can't say the word if I'm not one hundred percent sure that this is the man that jumped in my car last night. I don't want to send an innocent man to jail."

The detective said, "Trust us. He's not as innocent as you think. He has done a lot of things."

I could sense that I irritated the detective because it seemed like they just wanted me to say, "He's the one.'" They wanted to book him and put him in jail.

I said, "I have to be sure."

So they said, "Fine. We have some pictures for you to look at." That didn't help.

Then there was a lineup.

They said, "We're going to put him alongside some other guys and we need you to decide if this is the man or not. We really think it's the man."

They took me to the room to view the lineup. Right before I entered the room, the face of the guy from the night before flashed right before my face. Just like the lady told me that when the time was right, God would reveal it to me.

When I looked at the man in the lineup, I realized it was not the right man.

The person in lockup was not the man that had been in my car, but for some reason, I did feel that the wrong guy being arrested was experiencing a divine intervention that was necessary for him. It was as if he had done, or was about to do something he shouldn't have and this experience was going to help him straighten up and fly right.

The whole thing also stopped me from doing something that I shouldn't have been doing in the first place. It interrupted me from being with a guy, possible getting pregnant, or even catching an STD. Who knows? I was trying to hook up with Danny for the wrong reasons.

Now my car was totaled and I had to pay to repair the officer's car I hit. Well, actually my mother paid and I was grateful. I'm also grateful I am still alive. I'm healed, but there is always some degree of trauma when you experience something like that. For years, I would immediately lock my doors when I got in the car. Honestly, I still do.

I am more cautious in locking my doors. I'm more guarded and careful of talking to strangers. Even today, being in my car or anything with my doors unlocked is still not comfortable. I'm a little paranoid of that.

What did someone/people do that helped you?

The lady that came out of nowhere with her words of encouragement. I wonder if she was an angel coming to comfort me. Her peaceful voice, calm demeanor, and compassion for my well-being really meant a lot. I stopped crying just being able to talk to her.

I'm grateful the man got out of the other car with a gun to help. I'm grateful he had the courage to do it. He really thought we were trying to hurt him and he still responded.

What did someone/people do that disappointed you?

There are many women, before and after me, that have been put in that situation by someone touching them inappropriately or threatening their lives. There have been so many people carjacked, raped or even killed.

The neighbors that stayed behind their peepholes and watched the accident through their windows, heard me screaming, crying, saw me hanging out of the car, begging the driver of the car I hit for help, and they all waited until the crazy man ran off before they came out or called the police. They watched as if they had a bag of popcorn and they were watching at a movie.

What could someone/people have done that would have helped you?

The neighbors could have responded faster, and called for help, or just come out of their homes. I understand they were concerned for their own safety, but they could have done something. They could have called one another and decided to open their doors or make some noise to scare him off. There is power in numbers.

I knew, in spite of that man touching me and taking my jewelry, I was going to be okay. I just didn't know how it was going to play out. I knew God was with me.

Final Thoughts

I'm so different than that. If I see someone in distress, I immediately go into resolution mode. How can I help? What can I do? Whom can I call? I'm not going to just stand there watching. They need help. I would have tried to do something. Sometimes we have to take a stand boldly, especially when we know we have the protection of God in our lives. We have to stand up.

About the Victor:

Trisha Mann-Grant is a film/TV actress, producer, and author of *Amazing Testimonies*.

Trisha has been entertaining audiences since she was a little girl. Born and raised in Chicago, she grew up performing songs and skits in church. Since that time, the former Miss Black Chicago has graced the cover of many magazines and been a print model for *Ebony* and *Jet* magazines. She modeled and toured the country doing hair shows, national billboards and commercials for hair products. Her acting resume includes many musicals, stage plays, and television appearances.

Trisha is the creator and host of the radio show, Mann Talk.

She currently resides in Los Angeles, California, with her husband and fellow actor, Tony Grant, and her children.

"Whatever affects one directly, affects all indirectly. I can never be what I ought to be until you are who you ought to be. This is the interrelated structure of reality."

—Dr. Martin Luther King, Jr.

Change

We had a large home with a big back yard in a very affluent area in Sri Lanka.

My grandfather owned a very prominent shipping business. My grandmother raised five children and was well taken care of.

My father built our house with the intent of giving it to my mother, which is the norm in our culture. He believed you should buy the best of the best.

My mom was a stay-at-home mom with five girls. Similar to many other mothers, she liked to dress us alike. That usually meant a girly dress, but I was a tomboy and would have preferred to wear jeans and climb trees. That was frowned upon. My mom would get a lot of flack from relatives that she needed to get me in line, but she encouraged me to be me. (She didn't take their advice too often.)

Our life afforded us servants and a chauffeur. I remember him driving my dad around and taking my mom to the grocery store and us kids to school and back.

Our neighborhood was filled with politicians and very influential people. Dignitaries often visited.

My mother arranged lots of parties. They would sometimes be for business, but they would merge into a social party. Birthday parties were big. My dad would have a chef come in and the party would start on a Friday and end Sunday morning. It was a free time. Very island style.

That was my life from the time I was four until I was about nine.

Then, there was a gradual change. Things started happening, but they were always far away and in a remote area. A political unrest would happen here and there. The young people, mostly college age, would protest something they were unhappy about against the government. It was a bit of high unemployment on the island. Some of these well-educated students didn't want jobs they felt were beneath them. They wanted more.

That is where it started, mostly on college campuses. There was a faction group called the JVP, kind of like a hippie group. I forget what that stood for, but it was an acronym. That group was squashed, but the members quickly joined or created new groups. It started as a mostly peaceful group, but some of the students didn't agree on some things and they became a little more violent and aggressive in the split. I would compare it to the movement in the sixties in America with Dr. Martin Luther King, Jr., and Malcolm X. Part of what was driving this was our history. My country was colonized by Britain. We had been invaded by Portugal and other countries. We had never been self-governing. When we became independent, there were a lot of growing pains. It was the late '70s and early '80s, forty years into our independence. That whole generation had seen their parents come from an occupied or colonized environment and they wanted their own legacy.

Change

A lot of things were happening and my sisters and I were so young that we didn't quite understand.

It began to escalate when they began to take their protest from the remote area to the city. By the time I was ten, the protestors were threatening our daily way of life. They became terrorists. They would bomb a facility near a radio or television station so that it would be publicized. They would take hostages or even kill people and leave them in open areas to be discovered.

They began to threaten the schools that if you sent your children there, they would be harmed. In that area we wore uniforms so it was easy to spot students. You could define which school they were going to by the ties they wore or the color of the uniform. In an attempt to protect us, the schools closed.

Some of the affluent families had tutors. Others gathered together to home school, while others had nothing.

The parents still had to go to work. They didn't want to leave their children at home unattended. They began to send the children to school under false pretenses. They did not let them wear a uniform or go the normal route. They would have to sneak in to the school.

Our family, because we could afford it, was able to attend an accelerated underground program started by one of the biggest schools in the country. They created a two-year program. The schools are very advanced there. What you would do here in high school was typically done in our middle schools.

That does not mean we escaped danger. I remember one day in particular. My mom had the chauffer take her to the grocery store in the middle of the day. Because of where we lived, the terrorists knew who we were and our routine. The driver stopped at the gas station before heading to the store. As they continued, they were stopped by a terrorist group with guns and grenades. They stepped in front of the car. They wanted the gasoline. She knew she had been followed. She also knew what they intended to do with the gasoline. They were going to use it to burn bodies. This group felt the reason they didn't have employment or the same opportunities as others was because of another race within the nation. My country has Muslims, Tamils, Sinhalese, and Buddhists. There are Catholics, Protestants, and a lot of religions. This particular group of terrorists was blaming the Tamils and the Tamils were blaming them. There was a lot of back and forth racist bad blood.

Most of the affluent homes employed Tamils. Unlike the Tamils in the north, in the south the lower cast would accept meager jobs such as domestic work.

My mother knew these terrorists were known for kidnapping the Tamils, put tires around them and use the gasoline to set their bodies on fire. She did not want that on her conscience. So she put her body between the gas tank and the terrorist, and said, "If you want this gasoline, you're going to have to go through me." The chauffer tried to protect her. Even though she is only about five feet tall, she is strong and determined. She prevailed.

She believes God played a big part in protecting her that day. It had become normal practice for her to pray each time she left the house.

Change

This was not a normal occurrence, but the terrorists were becoming bolder and now infiltrating the city.

Around that same time, my cousin's house was invaded. They were taken hostage and their jewelry and cars were stolen.

My parents were trying to keep things from us because we were so young, but some of my cousins were our age and told us what happened.

The government implemented curfews. They suggested lights be turned off so the terrorists wouldn't know when we were home.

Because of the area we lived in, there were barricades where we had to show identification to cross. They needed to verify you lived in the area.

We had several people living with us at the time. Among them, my grandmother, my uncle (my mother's brother) who was like a cool big brother, and domestics, who were like our siblings.

One night there was a knock at the door. My uncle answered. It was the terrorists with huge machetes.

I remember the size of the blade, even though I just caught a quick glimpse. They put it to my uncle's neck and demanded he give them the Tamil servants. He told them we didn't have any. My grandmother got wind of what was happening and hid them throughout the house. They were like her children. They began in her household and were now in our household. They were like family.

I remember sitting on her bed and being afraid. What if they come in the house? What if they hold us hostage? She started telling us stories to keep us calm. She was always an active and creative person. She knit and sewed beautifully. I looked around and saw the needles and cloth. All the while we had people under the bed. We stayed there until it was safe.

My uncle came in to let us know the terrorists had left. They had taken food and some jewelry. It was as if you had to make a donation to further their cause even though you didn't agree with them. You just wanted them to leave. They knew they could come back another day for more.

We were under the impression they were following us. My grandmother's brother was a government official. It was well known that we were his family members.

That is when my parents decided it was time to sell the house and leave the country.

Before we could leave, there was an afternoon when no one was home or no one in the area where I was. On one side of our home there were several French doors. Against one of them was a big wicker lounge. I used to love to sit there and read. I read Nancy Drew mysteries, *Pride and Prejudice*, *Wuthering Heights*, and any series like those by C.S. Lewis. Reading was our escape since we were not allowed to go out very often anymore. We had to use our imagination. We had a big mirror in our bedroom and my sister told us that someone lived behind it like in *The Lion, The Witch, and The Wardrobe*, and we believed her. Anyway, it was a beautiful day. Then there was this massive bang. All of the French doors around me shook so hard. Whatever that boom was had to be very close by. I crouched over and covered my head and ears. I huddled in a mass. I thought if I could cover the front of my body, my back would be strong enough to survive.

Change

I knew that whatever happened next would be bad. I thought all of the doors behind me where going to come crashing down on top of me so I stayed in this huddled position. I didn't scream, but I held my breath. I'm sure my grandmother was somewhere, maybe upstairs, but the house was about four thousand square feet with a vestibule and a huge stairway, so as far as I was concerned, I was alone.

When the doors didn't collapse, I got up. There was still a vibration in the room, but nothing broke. God had saved me. I was in a large room with all windows and not one of them broke. When I went to the next room, there was a bar and a small window. That was the only window that cracked.

We later found that the bomb had occurred just up the street. The houses next door, in front, and behind ours were all badly damaged. Our house survived. It was divine intervention.

It's almost like an earthquake. You know they exist, but until you live through one it's hard to describe.

I remember I was wearing shorts. I know it sounds vain, but my legs were the one part of my body that I liked so I was protecting them.

I never felt unsafe in my home. My house had saved my life. I never thought about it before, but our house survived and kept us safe. I still have fond memories of that house.

When I left the house I felt at risk.

It was not just our family that was targeted so I didn't take it personally. Everyone was in danger.

Soon after that we began having family meetings about leaving. Because of my father's business, we had options. We were fortunate. I didn't realize that then. All I knew was that I didn't want to leave my friends.

Within the year we moved to Fremont, California.

A lot has transpired since that day, but my family and I survived. We have visited Sri Lanka, but we now reside in California and are US citizens. I really don't wish for anything to be different. Even though there are times I wish I had more time to spend with my extended family. My life is enriched today because of my experiences.

What did someone/people do that really helped you?

I don't know if I could say it was just one person, but my grandmother was a big positive. It was going to be a big change because all my family would not be leaving, just my immediate family. My mother did something unique. She put me in charge of the move. I was the nurturer. She said she needed my help. She gave me something to do.

What did someone/people do that really disappointed you?

I've let go of so many of those memories and some are blurred. I think my father played the executive card in making the decision to move the family. In hindsight, I understand, but then I thought he lacked empathy in what we were leaving. I thought, at age ten, I should have been consulted so I could protect my sisters. Again, that was my ten-year-old thinking. My dad and I were not very close.

Change

What could someone/people have done that would have helped you?

I think everyone could have explained what was happening and the haste of it. Sure, we gave it a lot of thought and there were many family discussions leading up to the move, but ultimately, my parents had to pull the trigger and say *let's go*. I wish we had stayed and fought. Given what I know now, and as a parent, I would have probably done the same thing for the safety of my child. But the ten-year-old tomboy wanted to stay and fight, even though I probably didn't understand the gravity of what or who I was fighting. Fortunately, we grew up speaking English and my mother insisted her girls take elocution and etiquette classes; my parents had high standards for their daughters. This prepared us to live in our new homeland.

About the Victor

Shan Fiske is the owner of Fiske Insurance Services. As a Manager and Benefits Specialist for years, she has an extensive portfolio of clients. Shan has experience working as a Corporate Cash Assistant Manager and Principal Financial Strategist for some of the largest financial firms in the country. She was an investment adviser and held licenses Series 7, 63, 24, 8, and 65. Shan has a heart to give and is involved with many charitable organizations. In business, she currently serves on several boards.

Shan resides in Aliso Viejo, California, with her husband of twenty years, Jon, and their son Matthew.

"Kind words can be short and easy to speak, but their echoes are truly endless."

—Mother Teresa

The Little Girl

In my family, there are two boys and two girls. I am the second child and the second girl. We were a rambunctious bunch. We were constantly talking one another into some crazy stunt that would get one, or all, of us in trouble with our mother. We tore our sheets and made tents in the bedrooms. My sister and I balled up our good sweaters, pinned them together and used receiving blankets to create our soft, newborn baby dolls to cradle. All of this activity marred items purchased for other purposes.

Once, we decided to throw the rinds from our watermelon in the air toward the top of the house to see who could throw the highest. The end result was four rather large rinds landing right on the edge of the roof. So of course we then had to throw toys, balls and anything else up there to try to knock the rinds down; none of which worked, but instead added to the roof's décor. My mother had gone to the store. When she pulled up in front of our house, saw the roof lined with watermelon rinds and toys, and her four little children standing there wide eyed, she couldn't do anything but laugh. I don't think she even asked any questions. She just solicited a neighbor to climb on the roof to retrieve our belongings and put the rinds in the trash.

We played, we fought. We kept secrets and covered one another; at other times we told on one another. Our alliance changed frequently to meet our current circumstances so you never knew what really happened. There was never a dull moment.

Now that school was out, we had all day to craft our neighborhood races or baseball games in the vacant lot at the corner, play football or have dance contests. In the early '70s, that was the norm. We didn't have computers or cell phones. We would begin each day with our chores and rush to get outside. That was where the fun was, outside. The parents on the block knew just where to find their children. We used our creativity and imagination.

It was a warm summer day. All of the children on the block were outside playing. As dusk became darkness, our parents began summoning each of us home.

"Five more minutes," we pleaded over and over.

After we exhausted all of our appeals, we finally relented and went inside. Time for the evening rituals.

There was nothing different about that particular evening. We were in the house watching television. We had dinner and cleaned the kitchen. It was my turn to take a bath. I gathered my pajamas and went to the bathroom. I ran my water while sitting on the toilet, with the top down, reading. I began to undress and then remembered my little brothers and thought I had better lock the door. It wouldn't have been unusual for them to run down the hall and open the door and run. I was eleven now and their childish pranks were annoying.

The Little Girl

I would yell, "Momma, tell them to stop! I'm trying to take a bath!"

Momma would say, "Will you leave your sister alone, please?"

I would be furious and they would be giggling.

Not this time. I locked the door.

I undressed and got in the tub. Being an avid reader, I would take my book with me and soak and relax.

I remember hearing a little noise. I looked around. I thought, *Not this time, you crazy boys, I locked the door.*

Then I heard the noise again. It seemed to be coming from the outside. I listened, but I wasn't too alarmed. There was a triplex next door and their side doors were on the same side as our bathroom window. I assumed it was a neighbor.

The noise got louder.

It seemed close. Closer than next door.

I was a little nervous, so I got out of the tub and had just put the towel around me when the bathroom window flew up. There was a man with a thick mustache staring at me.

With unimaginable horror, I screamed, "Momma!!"

My mother was immediately on the other side of the door. She kept asking what was wrong and she heard the terror in my voice, but I couldn't answer.

I just kept screaming, "Momma!!"

The man ran.

She was shaking the door handle. It was locked. She was trying to get me to unlock the door. I couldn't move. She told me to step back and she was trying to kick the door in.

I was shaking uncontrollably, but I managed to unlock the door.

She grabbed me and tried to comfort me.

I was crying and screaming, "He was trying to get in the house!"

She asked, "Who?"

"The man."

"What man?"

"The man in the window," I screamed, pointing to the window.

She went to the window and saw the screen had been removed and was on the ground.

She said, "Call the police. Call the police."

I don't remember who made the call, but if I had to guess, I would say my older teenaged sister. She had been in the kitchen sneaking to be on the phone with her boyfriend. She was on punishment and not supposed to be receiving or making calls. Her secret was revealed when he drove up like a superhero ready to save the day. He lived nearby, but certainly not close enough to have heard me scream. He admitted they were on the phone and he had heard me through the phone. My sister dropped the phone and ran to the bathroom door. He was on the other end asking, "What's happening? What's wrong?" When she didn't answer, he jumped in his car and drove over as fast as he could.

The police arrived.

They went outside and circled the house. There was no one there. They replaced the screen. They came in our home and began to ask me a lot of questions. I described everything.

The Little Girl

His face was etched into my memory.

One of my best friends lived on the next block. Our mothers were friends as well. They came over, too. I was still visibly shaken. My friend's mother suggested I go home with them that night. My mother asked me if I wanted to go and I very quickly agreed. There was no way I would sleep in that house that night.

Most of the other kids didn't know what had happened so I tried to appear as normal as possible. The next few weeks I played all the same games and laughed at the same jokes, but I had an awareness of every person that walked down our street. If I saw a man in the distance, I would run to my porch and stand right at the door until I was sure it was not him or until he passed by. If anyone would have been watching me, they would have seen the fear in my eyes. If they had held me, they would have felt my heart racing. If they were standing near me, I do believe they would have heard my heart pounding. I had anxiety, but I couldn't articulate that to anyone. I didn't want to be different, at least not in that way.

I thought *what if* he remembered me as well as I remembered him. *What if* he was coming back to hurt me so I couldn't identify him? *What if??? What if???* Would I ever be safe again?

Summer ended and I had made it. I celebrated my twelfth birthday and entered junior high school. I know today it's referred to as middle school, but not so back then. The following year we moved to a new neighborhood. That helped me a lot. Surely that awful man with the thick mustache would never find me. I excelled through the rest of my school years and even graduated a year ahead of my class. I think that experience made me sensitive to other children over the years. I hear what they say and what they don't.

That was over thirty years ago, and right now if I close my eyes, I can still see his face. I don't think about it anymore so it surprises me that I remember vividly so much of the details and the power of memory. I remember the entire ordeal and experience fresh sorrow. As I write this story, I cry for that little girl. Thank God she was so brave. Thank Him even more for protecting her.

What did someone/people do that helped you?

I think being at home when it happened and being surrounded by so many people that wanted to protect me was important. My mother was a fighter and you did not dare mess with her children. I knew she would keep me safe.

What did someone/people do that disappointed you?

Although everyone responded quickly, it did not last long enough. I don't think anyone realized the ongoing fear I was experiencing. They went back to their normal routines and I was stuck trying to rationalize things on my own.

What could someone/people have done that would have helped you?

Without a doubt, that would have been to watch me closer. I needed that feeling of protection. I didn't know how to ask for it, but all my actions silently requested it. I had been a very independent child and for a season I was a little clingy. I stayed a little closer to my mother or other adult family members.

Final Thoughts:

If you know, or suspect, that a child has experienced any type of trauma, don't just ask questions, watch. Watch their behavior. Watch to see if any of their normal responses have been altered. All too often we tell them to be a big girl or a big boy. They are not. They are children. That sentiment is fine if they fall while playing, but it is not enough to overcome trauma. They need affirmations to remind them that it was not their fault and that they will be protected to the best of your ability. They need that for as long as they need it. Each child is different. Do not allow a smile to lull you into thinking they are all better. Check again and again and again. You could save their emotional lives.

About the Victor:

She would like to remain anonymous. After all these years, she would rather leave that memory in the past. She felt compelled to share this story when she learned of the nature of this book. "I felt it was important because it speaks to the trauma of a child," said the victor, "and if reading this makes you ask one more time if they are okay or give a comforting embrace a little longer to provide security, then it was worth it."

Your Story

Now that you have read our stories of Valor 2 Victory perhaps you have a story of your own.

Take a moment to ask yourself if there is some memory in your past you have never told or is hindering you. Maybe there is something you always wished you had told. It may be a story you have told and you have seen how it has impacted others and you want to share here. We want to assist you.

Please describe your incident with as much detail as possible. Include every thought, feeling and emotion you can. You want people to visualize your story, to feel what you felt. In the words of Maya Angelou, "There is no greater agony than bearing an untold story inside you."

Tell your story in your own words.

_____
_____
_____
_____
_____
_____
_____

Valor 2 Victory

Your Story

Answer the following questions:

1. What did someone/people do that really helped you?

___

2. What did someone/people do that really disappointed you?

___

Valor 2 Victory

3. What could someone/people have done that would have helped you?

_____
_____
_____
_____
_____
_____
_____
_____
_____
_____
_____

Final Thoughts

Your final thoughts can be anything you would like to say. For example: How your experience impacted you, how you are today, or a summary of what you want people to learn from your experience.

> "Finally, my brethren, be strong in the Lord, and in the power of His might."
>
> —Ephesians 6:10

"You may not control all the events that happen to you, but you can decide not to be reduced by them."

—Dr. Maya Angelou

Acknowledgements

In addition to the wonderful people I mentioned in my story there are a plethora of others who championed me through this journey. I appreciate everyone that took the time to reach out and express kindness.

I'm grateful to my family for supporting me through a very challenging time. Thank you for providing a safe landing place that allowed me to share and receive love. I dare not try to name each of you so I will have no regrets by not including someone. I adore all of you. You are the joy in my life.

To my circle of ladies, you know who you are. We commemorate our lives by traveling together, meeting for birthdays and play dates. We experience adventures and take pleasure in the arts. We dine well and shop even better. We celebrate one another during our milestones and hold one another's hand in sorrow. We meet every December to pay tribute to another year together. Thank you for your prayers, calls, and cards. Thank you for being a part of my life.

Pastor Kenneth Mulkey, you have always been a confidant and a friend. Thank you for encouraging me through this ordeal and this project. I appreciate your wisdom and generosity. You are a man of integrity and generosity. Your love for God is contagious and it's no wonder He uses you globally to edify His kingdom.

Pastor Charles Belvin, when I needed a place to host a workshop educating people on how to respond when faced with trauma you opened your doors. Even though we had just met, you trusted me without hesitation. You took my calls when I needed someone to talk to (and you still do). You listen and always leave me feeling empowered. It's evident in your relationships at Lakewood Church International (LCI) that you really care about your church family. You are the epitome of a man after God's heart. Gaining you as a friend, mentor, and Bible teacher has been phenomenal. As you often tell me, "You don't' have to join to be a member". I say "Ditto". You are a member of my family too.

My buddy L.C. Green is a well-rounded family and business man, author, and entrepreneur. You have always been there supporting, encouraging and making me laugh. Your ability to see people, reach inside and pull the best out of them is brilliant. Your loyalty and consistent friendship is inestimable. I choose that word specifically for that best tax man in the biz.

To my victorious interviewees, thank you for sharing your experience and allowing me to share it in Valor 2 Victory. Your selfless act will undoubtedly impact the lives of many people. You are heroes and sheroes. May you be blessed beyond measure.

Jessica Wright Tilles, my editor and new friend. There are people wherein your first conversation you know you like them. They are talented and down-to-earth. You want the opportunity to grow together. That was my initial and continued response to

Acknowledgments

Ms. J. You did an amazing job and worked patiently with me. I can't wait to see where this *Valor 2 Victory* series takes us. Glad to have you onboard.

Awesome readers, my prayer is that one or all of these stories help you help someone. If you are the one in need, I pray you find encouragement in knowing you can survive and thrive. This series is for you.

To my Lord and Savior Jesus Christ, what can I say to an all-loving God that protected me, kept me and is still keeping me? Thank you, Abba. I will sing Your praises all the days of my life. I stand in awe of You.

www.ingramcontent.com/pod-product-compliance
Lightning Source LLC
Chambersburg PA
CBHW052026290426
44112CB00014B/2391